Scrum Mastery

Agile Leadership to Take Your Team's Performance from Good to Great

Jeff Cohn

The information in the following pages is broadly considered a truthful and accurate account of facts and as such, any inattention, use, or misuse of the information in question by the reader will render any resulting actions solely under their purview. There are no scenarios in which the publisher or the original author of this work can be in any fashion deemed liable for any hardship or damages that may befall them after undertaking information described herein.

Additionally, the information in the following pages is intended only for informational purposes and should thus be thought of as universal. As befitting its nature, it is presented without assurance regarding its prolonged validity or interim quality. Trademarks that are mentioned are done without written consent and can in no way be considered an endorsement from the trademark holder.

Table of Contents

Introduction...5

Chapter 1: What makes a great Scrum Master?...........10

Chapter 2: Anti-patterns in Scrum and Agile 34

Chapter 3: Establishing effective team mechanics 56

Chapter 4: Building a high-performance team...........80

Chapter 5: Getting everyone on board... and
      keeping them there..102

Chapter 6: Running a sprint.......................................118

Chapter 7: Scaling up Scrum 140

Conclusion 158

Introduction

Thank you for choosing, *"Scrum Mastery. Agile leadership to take your team's performance from good to great."* If you are reading this, it is because you are serious about getting the most out of what Agile and Scrum have to offer you and your organization.

If you are new to the world of Agile, I would encourage you to check out the previous volume to this book entitled, *"Scrum Fundamentals. A beginner's guide to mastery of the Scrum project management methodology."* In it, you will find a trove of information and knowledge regarding the worlds of Scrum and Agile.

Also, you will learn more about how Scrum and Agile can fit your organization so that you can run your projects, and your company as whole, under the "Agile mindset." This is a very useful approach as it will enable you to focus on delivering value to your customers while empowering your team to be at its best.

If you are experienced in the world of Agile and Scrum, then you have come to the right place. While there are other books available on this subject, you will be hard pressed to find a single tome that can deliver the amount of information and practical examples that you will find here.

Consequently, I would like to encourage you to take your time with this book. This isn't the type of book which you can just breeze through and be done with it. Since it is packed with information and actionable advice, you will surely find something new every time you go through it. I have taken great care in making sure that you have everything you need in order to get the most out of your use of Scrum and Agile in your organization.

So, when building upon the fundamentals of Agile and Scrum, many practitioners run into some dead ends. For instance, may Scrum practitioners are clear on the underlying philosophy regarding the methodology itself, but may be unclear as to the actual roles of the main players in Scrum. While the role of Scrum developers is generally straightforward, the role of the Scrum Master and the Product Owner tends to be a bit more complex to understand.

The reason for this is that traditional project management methodologies espouse a much more rigid and hierarchical structure in which the main focus of the leadership roles is to direct and coordinate activities. There is a clear pecking order which must be respected. Moreover, leadership roles in a traditional project management environment aim to establish clear roles for responsibility and competence.

Within the Agile mindset, responsibility is shared across the team. Therefore, one person is not "responsible" for the project. Rather, the entire team is responsible in such a way that they are tasked with pushing the project through to the end. In addition, the credit for the project's success is also evenly distributed among all of the members of the team. This not only breeds empowerment, but it also breeds a sense of satisfaction and success.

Another of the most important elements that will be discussed in this book is how to build a successful Scrum team. Often, practitioners don't have a clear perspective as how to a successful Scrum team can be built. As such, a lack of understanding in this regard may lead to complex situations that lead to failure.

Therefore, it is crucial that you, as a Scrum practitioner, have a clear understanding of the methodology and how that methodology relates to the overall mechanics of a successful

Scrum team. So, we will drill down into the mechanics of a successful Scrum team insofar as determining best practices, based on experience, which can help you gain the right edge in the world of Agile project management.

As such, your understanding of Scrum and Agile will enable you to develop the right types of patterns and behaviors which will foster communication and an overall sense of accomplishment in your team. As your team gains more traction, they will develop a greater sense of empowerment. This will not only lead to a higher level of motivation, but also to a higher level of self-satisfaction. Thus, this creates a feedback loop which cannot be compared to anything else.

One other vital element that will be dealt with in this book is the scaling of Scrum. In the previous book, we touched on how Scrum is not just limited to one team, one Scrum Master and one Product Owner. Scrum can be scaled up as much as needed. That means that regardless of a project's scope and requirements, Scrum is able to address project objectives in such a way that project deliverables can be met on time and with the desired quality.

Naturally, large scope projects utilizing Scrum as its underlying project management methodology do require more careful planning and coordination, but that is true of any project under any methodology. Thus, it's vital that project leaders do their best to make sure that every project component is in its rightful spot.

So, as we are set to begin, it's important to keep an open mind. I know that this book will challenge your previous notions on project management, including what you may have already seen and read about Scrum and Agile. That is why our intent is to provide you with greater insight into what the latest Scrum and Agile practices have to offer project management professionals, or virtually any professional in the realm of business administration.

I am sure that the insights which you will find in this book will be useful both in your daily management practices, as well as, any project you would be looking to coordinate. Please bear in mind that there is no project too big, or too small, to have an appropriate measure of Scrum incorporated into it.

So, let's get started with this discussion. We have quite a bit to talk about. And, I am sure you are as eager as I am to get the ball rolling.

Chapter 1: What makes a great Scrum Master?

When you think of a Scrum Master, what comes to mind?

Is it:

a. An all-knowing sage who is a Scrum encyclopedia
b. The fearless leader who knows exactly what to do at all times
c. The project manager who is in charge of all operations
d. "The boss"

If you picked any of the above answers, you'd be wrong.

In the Agile world, leadership is not about being the boss, being right or having the power. Within the Agile domain, being in a leadership position means you are there to help your team win any way possible.

So, "win" is the operative word in this discussion.

Often, folks who come up through the ranks in the project management profession feel they are entitled to having control, power or any other type of dominance over the way the project is carried out. In fact, this is true of projects run under a traditional project management style in which the last thing that people are looking for in the team work, but rather, just getting the job done.

Consequently, being a leader in the Agile and Scrum world means that you need to check your ego at the door. If you are able to let your ego sit in the backseat, then you will have a great chance to lead your team in such a way that they will be successful.

So, what is all of this talk of Agile and Scrum?

If you are new to the world of Agile project management methodology, I would encourage you to drill down and really get a feel for the underlying philosophy that supports the entire Agile movement.

If you are a grizzled veteran of the Agile world, then I am sure you can come to appreciate the finer points of the underlying philosophy that holds up the entire Agile world.

Agile is all about getting things done as best as possible and as quickly as possible. It is really that simple. There are no gimmicks or tricks. The underlying philosophy that supports Scrum is good, old-fashioned team work and elbow grease.

There are no secret mantras that your team needs to chant before starting the day.

There are no special formulas to making things happen.

All there is, is a solid foundation which enables your team to work under clear guidelines and rules. So, you are essentially taking the guesswork out of your project management approach. What you are doing is enabling your people to make their own decisions based on their own sound judgment and understanding.

A brief history of Agile

Agile isn't exactly new, but it hasn't been around for too long, either. In fact, the concept of Agile was born out of the disgruntled nature of software developers that couldn't find a proper approach to apply to their software development projects.

The fact that developers were unhappy about traditional project management approaches led to a group of 11 software engineers come together to develop the Agile manifesto.

The Agile manifesto is the document with the underlying philosophy supporting the entire Agile movement. It is a conceptual framework which places the onus on the team working on the project management and not the almighty leader who has all the answers and bears the entire responsibility for the success, or failure, of the project.

The most important aspect of the Agile manifesto is the shift in mindset from a hierarchical structure, to a flat one in which the customer takes center stage while the team is left to organize itself in a collaborative manner.

As such, here is the actual text of the Agile manifesto as conceived by its creators:

We are uncovering better ways of developing software by doing it and helping others do it. Through this work we have come to value:

Individuals and interactions over processes and tools

Working software over comprehensive documentation

Customer collaboration over contract negotiation

Responding to change over following a plan

That is, while there is value in the items on the right, we value the items on the left more.

As you can see from the Agile manifesto itself, the focus is on delivering value at all times. Value is what drives the production of software in such a way that it consistently delivers value to customers at all stages of the project.

Notice how the Agile manifesto makes a point of highlighting "individuals and interactions" and not processes. Also, it values working software over documentation while encouraging collaboration over contracts. Finally, responding to change is the key element as compared to following a plan.

Definitely, Agile espouses as a methodology which is flexible and dynamic so that project teams are consistently focused on embracing change rather than sticking to a rigid plan at all costs. As such, change is the number one item on the minds of all Agile project managers.

Now, one of the mot common objections to Agile methodologies is that it has been specifically designed for the software industry. And while it is true that it was born out of the software industry, it has since grown to a much more cross-cutting appeal in which it can be applied in several industries and not just software development.

Later on in this book, we will get a chance to dig deeper into how Scrum and Agile can be implemented in virtually any type of industry and not just software or IT. Most importantly, the Agile mindset is a fundamental shift in the overall perception a company has of its methods and means of running the business.

That being said, it's important to focus on the fact that Agile is not about implementing a technology that will solve all of the challenges that project managers face on a regular basis. While it does create a discipline within project management as a whole, Agile is not about developing the perfect system; it's about creating an environment which is conducive to success.

Three pillars of Scrum

Given the fact that Agile, and consequently Scrum, are all about empowering project team members and providing value to customers, it is only fitting that the three pillars of Scrum are based on three core principles centered around people:

1. Transparency
2. Inspection
3. Adaptation

These principles are rooted in enabling individuals to take control over their tasks and responsibilities in such a way that there is a maximization of output through collaborative endeavors.

As such, each of the pillars that make up Scrum project management methodology are a direct spin off Agile. Thus, it is important to note that Agile is the overarching framework which Scrum is based on. These pillars are a direct representation of how Agile is conceived and how Scrum can be implemented to suit the needs of individual projects.

Transparency

The first pillar is transparency.

And, needless to say, this one is a biggie.

Transparency is one of the most important factors that plays into effective Scrum implementation and accountability is an especially big deal.

Now, traditional project management methodologies espouse having a project manager who bears the ultimate responsibility of a project's success. If the project bears the results it was intended to, then the project manager is a hit. If the project fails, the project manager is the one to blame.

This approach creates a single point of accountability which virtually zaps any potential for growth and innovation on the part of individual team members. In fact, under a traditional approach, individual members are seen as interchangeable pieces which can be replaced as needed.

Indeed, this is a clear reflection on management philosophies and practices which are not conducive to a collaborative environment. By the same token, the project manager needs to supervise and make sure that everyone does everything they are supposed to be doing. This not only drains time and attention away from actual work, but it can also lead to attrition both on the part of the team members and project manager.

This is where Scrum offers a fantastic alternative. Scrum draws from the Agile manifesto and places greater importance on people rather than processes. This entails that understanding what each team member brings to the table becomes a vital component of determining the broader approach the Scrum team can utilize in a project.

When a collaborative, self-organizing approach is encouraged, team members are much more motivated and willing to find the best way to get the job done. Often, this leads to innovation and alternate solutions to complex problems.

Collaborative teams allow everyone to pitch in on equal terms while allowing the sum of the forces to multiply their efforts. Of course, being self-organizing also implies being that each team member needs to be accountable for their actions and their role on the team.

This is where transparency becomes such a key issue. Here, transparency pertains to individual team members within the team's dynamic, but it also refers to transparency with the customer. Since Scrum continuously produces "working software", the customer can see the direction the final product is taking at various stages of the project. This is where customers have the opportunity to see if the path the final product is taking truly meets their expectations.

Inspection

The second pillar refers to inspection. However, inspection does not refer to the traditional manufacturing type of inspection in which outputs are carefully scrutinized in order to determine where potential defects may lie.

Sure, Scrum advocates close review of outputs in order to ensure that they comply with customer specifications, but the fact of the matter is that inspection is part of a broader process of continuous improvement. What that means is that Scrum teams are always in search of improving processes and outputs. Therefore, it is crucial to have a clear understanding of what issues may arise with the actual implementation of the final solution.

Scrum also enables all members of the team to keep track of the entire team's work. This implies that each member has the opportunity to see what everyone else is doing at any given point in time.

Does this mean that anyone can inspect the work being done?

Yes, however, the point is not to be overly critical of the work being done. Rather, this affords everyone the opportunity to see how their work fits within the grander scheme of things. Based on that, individual members may be able to pick up on something which may have been overlooked by the rest of the team.

It is also important to understand that individual team members must be open-minded in the sense that feedback is intended to improve and not to criticize for the sake of criticism. The feedback that comes from both the team itself and the customer is intended to address the potential issues that may arise throughout project development. This allows for a proactive approach focused on developing trust and confidence among all project stakeholders.

Adaptation

The third pillar refers to dealing with change.

In any project context, change is one of the most common issues that project teams must face.

Change is inevitable. There is nothing that can be done to stop change. Change will happen as naturally as night and day. The issue then becomes how to deal with such change.

Traditionally, one of the aims of project management is to reduce the amount of uncertainty and change in projects in order to make them as predictable as possible. The reasoning behind this attitude is that project managers face constant pressure with regard to sticking to schedules and budget. There is nothing worse in the project management world than to have a project run over schedule and over budget. This not only speaks negatively on the project manager and team, but it also implies that the project wasn't planned properly.

Nevertheless, it is not always a question of planning and lack of management skills that may cause a project to go haywire. In fact, there are n number of possibilities which would cause a project to go off the rails. As such, the issue does not lie with individual problems. Rather, it lies with the way these individual issues are dealt with.

Detractors and critics of Scrum often point to the reactionary nature of adapting to change. And yes, that is true: a great deal of what Scrum advocates is reacting to change as it happens, or as it is requested. But the truth of the matter is that adaptability in Agile and Scrum lies at the very core of its conceptual framework.

Often, experienced Scrum teams will be able to anticipate issues and thereby implement change solutions before the potential issue actually becomes an issue. This is one of the most important virtues that change management has under the Scrum umbrella.

At the end of the day, Scrum Masters are encouraged to aid their team in identifying potential risks so that issues may be addressed early on in the sprint rather than at any other point in the process.

Being a great Scrum Master

So, this brings us back to the original point in this chapter: what makes a great Scrum Master?

In short, a great Scrum Master is only as good as their team.

This implies that leadership in Agile is not about being superior, but rather, it is about serving others. I know that may seem a bit counterintuitive with the traditional concept of leadership. In fact, most management programs call for leaders to be the fearless guide that has all the answers.

Even in more progressive management training programs, leaders in the Agile domain are considered to be superior in all aspects to their team members. This is a requisite trait that is needed in order to "earn" the respect of peers.

The truth of the matter is that the term "Scrum Master" refers to the level of mastery an individual has in Scrum methodology, but not in terms of being a "master" of some domain. In fact, Scrum Masters have a dual role.

First, Scrum Masters are expected to provide guidance and leadership to their team while allowing their team to find the best way to implement the methodology as prescribed by best practices.

Second, Scrum Masters are known as "subservient leaders." What this means is that a Scrum Master should not be bossing everyone around making sure things get done. On the contrary, the role of the Scrum Master is to ensure that their team has everything they need in order to get the job done.

This sounds more like a coordination role. In fact, it is. A Scrum Master is a coordinator who is in charge of making sure that everything is being done the way it is supposed to be done.

But, wait a minute, that sounds like a boss.

Not in the traditional sense.

A good Scrum Master is able to "direct traffic" in such a way that all of the players on the team know where they are going and how to get there. Since teams are self-organizing, the Scrum Master is basically on the sidelines acting like a coach.

This implies that when the Scrum Master detects something that is not going according to plan, they have the prerogative of bringing it up at meetings. This is part of the Scrum feedback loop that is intended at developing appropriate mechanisms and procedures.

The three platinum principles

Therefore, leadership in Agile and Scrum is based on the three platinum principles.

These principles, much like the three pillars, are intended to provide a road map for all team members to follow. While it is true that there may be more than one way to achieve similar results, the fact of the matter is that it is vital for all team members to go in the same direction. This will ensure that efforts are concentrated on where they matter most. Most importantly, the direction the team takes will be determined by the team itself. As such, the road travelled should be one with which each team member is comfortable.

Consequently, the three principles are listed as follows:

1. Resisting formality
2. Thinking and acting as a team
3. Visualizing rather than writing

On the surface, these principles might seem rather counterintuitive. They don't necessarily adhere to what is considered "normal" in the business world. Thus, we need to take a closer look at each one of these principles.

Resisting formality

This first principle really stands out.

What does it mean to "resist formality"?

It might sound like the team will walk around in their pajamas all day playing video games while they work.

Formality, in an Agile sense, is about a rigid structure which cannot be modified for anything in the world. As such, Agile frowns upon having set structures which do not foster creativity and embrace change. Thus, formality is seen as valuing processes over people. Consequently, the spirit of Agile is not being fully embraced.

Being Agile is all about breaking down barriers and finding solutions to problems and challenges which may have posed a considerable risk in the past. For instance, the phrase, "it's always been that way" is a huge no-no in the Agile mindset.

Therefore, Scrum teams are encouraged to push the envelope and test traditional assumptions. If something has always been done in a certain way, then perhaps it's time to try something new. After all, innovation leads to breakthroughs which can significantly alter the course of things.

As for the Scrum Master, "formality" refers to the being the "almighty" leader who is always right. In fact, the true role of the Scrum Master challenges all assumptions of what leadership should be in the business world. As a matter of fact, leadership under this context is exerted by exhibiting the traits that make a team successful rather than just issuing orders.

Thinking and acting as team

The second principle harkens back to the collaborative nature of Scrum.

The name "Scrum" was conceived from Rugby. In this sport, all of the players on the field act a whole since the action never stops. Once the ball is put into play, the two teams battle for control of the ball. Once one team has control, they must all work together in order protect each other from their opponents and eventually reach the other end of the field.

This is exactly what Scrum is all about.

The fact that the Scrum methodology calls for teamwork, that implies that any one team member may have the ball at any time, but must also be ready to pass it off to the next player. Once a team member has passed off the ball, then their role is to protect the player with the ball. In this type of approach, there is no waiting on one side of the field in order to "get open."

In this approach, you must be both open and ready to protect your teammates at all times.

Hence, Agile leaders are all about fostering teamwork. Teamwork is seen as the core attitude which will make projects successful. If teamwork cannot be encouraged, then it is safe to say that the project will be met with considerable headwinds.

Does this mean that a lack of teamwork will doom a project?

Not necessarily.

What it does mean is that adequate teamwork will make everyone's lives a lot easier. That is why the Scrum Master should focus on building a close-knit team. This can be achieved through a number of actions. But regardless of how it is achieved, it is up to the Scrum Master to make sure that any potential issues among team members are to be dealt with immediately. The last thing a Scrum Master wants is to have personal differences get in the way of the collaborative nature of the project.

Visualizing rather writing

The third platinum principle ties in with the Agile concept of "working software over comprehensive documentation."

Sure, all projects need to have certain details in black and white. In fact, it would be

29

irresponsible to commit things to memory while leaving agreements and accords as simple words.

However, this does not mean that teams should focus their efforts on producing manuals, handbooks, and reports. Scrum teams are successful at visualizing what the best solution is and how any potential solution can lead to improving the quality of the output. Thus, Scrum Masters are also tasked with helping the project team visualize what the best solution for the team would be. That is, what the best way of doing something would be.

This is a solution that only the team can develop. The Scrum Master needs to resist the temptation of imposing their will on the team. Naturally, the Scrum Master has valuable input as to what the team may or may not be able to do. But ultimately, the way things are done is a collaborative team decision.

This implies that leadership within Agile must look toward building a consensus on the approach that a project will take on while ensuring that team members have everything they need in order to make that vision happen.

Bringing it all together

At this point, I am confident that you have a good understanding of how Scrum and Agile conceive project management. Nevertheless, it is also important to bring everything together in a practical example.

I recall an experience I had some time ago.

There was a very bright young lady who was at the helm of a project which utilized Scrum. This young lady was in charge of bringing the team together and setting them up for success. She was totally committed to building her team on Agile principles.

Once the team was assembled, she asked everyone to "check their egos at the door" (she actually said that). She made the point that everyone was equally good. This wasn't a team with one good player and a supporting cast. This was a team of stars.

She was also clear that her role was to facilitate and coordinate the actions among all team members. Her job was to make sure that everyone understood what the project was about, and how each, individual member could use their talents in achieving the project outcomes.

After the work breakdown was determined, team members distributed tasks among themselves based on who was better suited for each task. The team quickly divided the work up amongst themselves and got to work.

The Scrum Master stood in the background monitoring progress and making sure that everyone stayed on track. She would have regular one-on-one chats with all members in addition to the regular daily meeting.

These one-on-one sessions were not about sitting down and having a formal review. These were just informal chats about how things were going and if there were any issues that each developer faced. More often than not, questions would arise about methodology, how to do something, and the best way to do it.

Whenever a team member did not know how to do something, or perhaps wasn't sure about the best way to do it, the Scrum Master would pose the question to the team. Sure enough, someone knew the answer.

While the execution of this project was not perfect, the attitude of the Scrum Master had been. She was clear that her role was to support her team at all times while ensuring that everyone felt valued and appreciated.

In the end, the project hit all its targets on time. The customer was thrilled with the results. It was a successful project that owed its success to the positive attitude of all team members and the selfless nature of its project lead, the Scrum Master.

Chapter 2: Anti-patterns in Scrum and Agile

In the first chapter of this book, we took an in-depth look at what leadership in Agile is and the specific role a Scrum Master plays within a Scrum project.

We also understood the collaborative nature of Agile in such a way that Scrum teams are driven by teamwork and not individual success. Often, individuals lose sight of the fact that individual performance is augmented by team success rather than the other way around.

Sure, there are sports, industries, companies, endeavors, and so on, which are driven by one individual. Think of a great sports star such as Michael Jordan.

Michael Jordan was the centerpiece of the Chicago Bulls NBA dynasty in the 1990s. However, Michael Jordan could never have won all of those championships without the help of his teammates. The likes of Scottie Pippen, Dennis Rodman and Steve Kerr, to name a few, were instrumental in helping the Bulls to six championships during Michael Jordan's career.

Does that mean that the aforementioned players were a supporting cast of characters which helped him reach success? Actually, they were equal. Except they played different positions. Moreover, when Jordan wasn't having a good game, was hurt, or was under intense pressure from the other team, it was his teammates who picked up the slack and led the team.

This a great example of what Scrum is all about. The Scrum team members are individuals who are good, if not the best, at what they do. They are adept at making things happen and getting the job done. They are able to work together and come up with the best possible solution to their customer's requests.

However, nothing good comes without its caveats.

In Scrum, as with any other project management methodology, there is always the risk of things not going right. It might be something simple which can be addressed immediately. But if left unattended, it may fester and grow into a larger issue.

Or, the project may be facing considerable headwinds and the project team needs to rally together in order to get the job done. When such circumstances occur, teamwork becomes paramount in overcoming such headwinds.

The Scrum Master, more than ever, acts like the Bulls' legendary coach Phil Jackson, standing on the sidelines making sure the team is working well together and picking up on things that perhaps the team itself may not be aware of.

This collaborative attitude ensures that team members stay focused and in sync with everything happening around them. As such, the Scrum Master is hardly the star. They are just ensuring that the coordination done among the team works perfectly.

Nevertheless, there are several pitfalls that Scrum practitioners need to pay attention to. These are called "anti-patterns" as they go against the prescribed Agile methodology. So, in this chapter, we will take a closer look at how these anti-patterns may develop, and how they may end up dragging the team down and holding back optimal results.

Not updating progress

The first of the anti-patterns in this chapter pertains to not tracking and updating progress.

I have decided to tackle this topic first as there is much to talk about.

Tracking progress is one of the essential functions in any project management methodology. Progress, in simple terms, can be tracked by the number of tasks completed.

Also, a broader measure of success can be seen in the number of objectives, or in the case of Scrum, user stories, completed.

Tracking progress has both an administrative and psychological function.

Firstly, it is an administrative function

since tracking progress allows the team to see what has already been achieved and what is left to do. This is the right way in order to determine how far along the project is and if the remaining tasks will be met within the time frame that was established at the outset of the project or individual sprint.

When the team is clear on the progress that is being made, all team members can feel confident in the work they are doing. Motivation is increased, as there is a greater sense of satisfaction in the work being done.

Secondly, it is also a psychological factor since it allows the team to see the finish line getting closer.

Think of it this way: you are a sailor on a ship that has been at high seas for a long time. You may feel discouraged and even desperate at the thought of there being nothing else around you except water. This can lead to a sailor flipping out and becoming mad. Believe me, sailors went through this back in the day.

Now, imagine for a second that you see land. After all that time at sea, you finally get a glimpse of land. Sure, land may still be very far away, but you have your first sight of the finish line.

So, tracking progress is much the same way. Of course, I don't intend to make a Scrum sprint seem like being at sea for countless days. The point that I want to drive home is the fact that tracking progress allows team members to find their bearings and become confident in the fact that their work is counting for something.

Under Scrum methodology, it is the Scrum Master's job to make sure that progress is being tracked accordingly. Sure, it's up to the entire team to make sure that there is a proper track of everything that is being completed throughout the project, but the ultimate responsibility of tracking progress is up to the Scrum Master.

As such, Scrum utilizes the "board" to track progress.

A Scrum board is a visual device which measures the progress of the tasks being completed This board intends to provide a visual representation of the tasks being completed and the ones which are still in progress.

So, the issue does not lie in the failure to update the board as such, but rather, in the failure to track progress. Of course, you might think that it doesn't matter if the board is not update because everyone is on the same page on what they are doing.

Well, you might be wrong. In fact, not tracking progress can lead to a team falling behind since they don't know where they clearly stand. Also, the team may lose focus on what they are truly meant to do. Thus, failure to track progress will lead to teams duplicating tasks or missing tasks altogether simply because they don't have the input they need in order to follow up on their progress.

Finally, the failure to track progress speaks on how the leadership in the project is committed to the overall project. In essence, it means there is a high degree of disregard for the project itself and the level of commitment that the leaders, in this case the Scrum Master, have for their role in the project.

So, the Scrum Master needs to be fully committed to seeing the project come to fruition. By being fully committed, the Scrum Master will be sure to follow through on their tasks in addition to encouraging their team to follow through on theirs. This breeds excellence in the way tasks are conducted throughout the lifecycle of the project.

Taking on work outside of the sprint

Each sprint should be a carefully planned exercise.

At the outset of each sprint, the Sprint Planning Meeting serves as the means by which the Scrum Master and the Development Team (this meeting may also include the participation of the Product Owner) define the scope of the sprint in order to determine the amount of tasks that will be completed, in addition to defining which tasks will be completed and which ones may be left over for ensuing sprints.

Now, during the Sprint Planning Meeting, prioritization should be given to requisite tasks, that is, tasks that need to be completed in order for future tasks to build on. This implies that requisite tasks get a higher prioritization as compared to other tasks which may contribute to the completion of a user story but may not necessarily be completed in that particular sprint.

When work is carefully delineated, the Scrum team is focused and engaged on what needs to be done. The Scrum team keeps track of the work completed and the work remaining to be done. This provides a discipline for the work that is to be done throughout the sprint.

However, what happens when change comes into the picture?

If there is a request for change on the part of the customer or even the Product Owner, the Development Team must find a way to incorporate those changes into future sprints especially since the current sprint cycle has work that has already been planned and assigned.

But what is the big deal with taking on work that was not originally planned in the sprint?

You see, the problem is not taking on additional work as such. The problem is the additional work means that time, attention and resources will be deviated from the originally planned tasks into new tasks which may not necessarily contribute to the objectives of that specific sprint.

In fact, there are cases where the user stories and tasks planned at the beginning of the sprint were not the right ones. That may even lead to the cancellation of a sprint (more on that later on). The fact remains that doing something "extra" may hinder your team's chances of getting valuable work done.

Consider this: the client has requested additional features or functionalities which weren't part of the original plan. So, the Product Owner sits down with the client and makes them see that this implies additional work not contemplated during the project planning phase. The client agrees with this and also agrees to pay extra for the additional work requested.

What do you do in this case?

First, the wrong answers.

You decide to see in which sprints you can fit the additional work requested and ask your team to incorporate it into their planning. After all, you need to meet the project's deadline as agreed upon at the beginning of the project itself.

While this solution may seem logical on the surface, you would be overloading your team. What happens is that you have already planned the number of sprints it would take to achieve the project outcomes. So, if you decide to take on more work within the same time frame, then you would be over extending your team.

By doing this, you may end up missing deadlines and thereby your targets. You may incur in cost and time overruns. Ultimately, you could jeopardize the entire project's integrity. So, you would need to carefully plan incorporating new tasks into the sprints you have already designed.

Also, you could hire more team members. On the whole this may actually work. You might be able to pull it off if you are able to find someone who can complete the new tasks during the actual time your project is underway.

Now, there is something to be said about bringing new team members in mid-project or mid-sprint. If you find yourself needing to add more team members or having to replace members, it's best to do this at the beginning of a new sprint and not mid-way. Sure, there might be extenuating circumstances in which you have to do this. For example, you might lose a team member due to a sudden illness and there is no reasonable way the other team members can pick up the slack.

In fact, there may be such circumstances in which you may end up having to cancel the sprint altogether as the team may lose a significant amount of members. This is hardly the ideal case, but you would certainly have to consider it rather than drag on a sprint that would lead to poor results.

The right answer in this case would be to add a sprint, or multiple sprints, in order to accommodate for the new requirements. If the customer is aware of the fact that they are requesting changes which were not a part of the original planning, then the customer should also agree to having additional sprints created in order to account for the additional work that will be done.

This is an important aspect that needs to be taken into account since additional features and functionalities means additional work. It is really that simple. So, it pays to be clear on what change requests imply to you and your Development Team.

No "work in progress" limit

A work in progress is just that, a work in progress.

However, when does a work in progress become a target which was not achieved?

This is a fair question to consider. After all, there is a logical point in which a task that was not completed becomes a task that was failed to be achieved.

This implies the need to set a boundary at which the "work in progress" becomes a "work not done."

There are a couple of ways of approaching this.

Firstly, the "work in progress" designation applies only to those tasks which were not completed during the sprint. If a task is yet to be completed at the end of a sprint, then it should be deemed a "work not done." This designation means that the team failed to achieve this objective.

So, at the Sprint Retrospective Meeting, the Scrum Master and the Development Team (with the participation of the Product Owner), can go over the reasons why the task was not achieved and how this could have been avoided.

Of course, the number of reasons why a task is not completed can be numerous. But the fact of the matter is that the Development Team needs to have a firm understanding of where things went wrong, and why it is necessary to understand this for the sake of future sprints.

Furthermore, the Scrum team can now decide if the task will be included in an upcoming sprint or dropped altogether. This is important to consider as the team may have decided to include a task which was not needed or perhaps planned too much work.

If the team took on too much work at the outset of the sprint, then the team may choose to revise the ways in which it decides what tasks to include and the amount of time needed to complete them. If the task was unnecessary, then the team must understand why it was included in order to avoid including needless tasks in the future.

Since Scrum is all about getting work done efficiently, then including work that is not needed may result in highly inefficient project management. As such, it's a rather clear reason why Scrum teams should not take on any work that wasn't originally intended in a sprint.

Of course, there is nothing wrong with admitting that a task was not completed and therefore needing to determine where and when it must be completed. The main point here is knowing and understanding that there is a point when the task is an official "failure."

So, it is up to the Scrum Master and even the Product Owner to sit down during the Sprint Retrospective Meeting and go over the reasons why the sprint failed to deliver such results. Ultimately, being able to understand and determine where the problem took place will create a very good discipline for the team moving forward.

One other important note about work in progress limits. Often, project teams have the initiative to add on features and functionalities which the customer did not request, but that they feel would be beneficial to the project.

Now, it's one thing to correct a potential problem and it's another to do something you feel the customer will like. This approach is just asking for trouble. If you are adding features which the customer did not request, that will only lead to extra work being done, which was not contemplated at the beginning of the sprint, but that end up altering the scope of the project.

Sure, you might think that if you have some time left over you can get around to it. Well, it is not about filling up left over time. If you have more time left over at the end of the sprint, you can always use that time to test the product and make sure that everything is working the way it is supposed to. If you detect any bugs, you can take that time to work them out and correct any issues beforehand.

Bear in mind that by being focused and sticking to what you committed to, you will please your customer by delivering on your word and making sure that you have exactly what they need, when they need it. That is efficiency.

At the end of the day, the Product Owner needs to manage change in order to ensure that any change requests, either don't fall outside of the scope of the project or delay the final delivery of the product.

For instance, the customer decides that they don't like the layout and color schemes of a software application. So, they request changes to the layout. This may result in delaying the final delivery of the application by a certain amount of time. At that point, the customer needs to be aware that that change will delay the product's completion.

Also, if a customer realizes they want something else added to the product which they suddenly thought it needed, the Product Owner can negotiate to have it tacked on to the end of the sprint cycle. This will avoid overburdening the project team with unnecessary tasks that will lead them to missing deadlines and racking up uncompleted tasks.

So, it certainly pays to be clear with the customer about what change requests mean and how they can impact the overall completion of the project.

Not cancelling a bad sprint

This one is a biggie.

We have talked about cancelling a sprint throughout this chapter. But, can you really cancel a sprint?

Of course!

However, it should be noted that we are not talking about cancelling a sprint just because something went wrong. Cancelling a sprint should be seen as a last resort type of situation.

So, under which circumstances should a sprint be cancelled?

Let's consider some practical situations.

Firstly, you have a Development Team consisting of 6 members. The team is underway with a sprint when suddenly one team member has fallen ill. They are sick and cannot come into work for at least a couple of weeks. Given that you have a four-week sprint, that's basically half the sprint. So, your team decides to suck it up and divide the tasks among the remaining five members.

At this point, you feel that you may have to work some overtime, but you can get the job done. The rest of the team is willing to pick up the slack and get the job done. So, you keep moving. But what happens if you lose another team member for whatever reason?

All of a sudden you are now down to four members doing the work of six. In this case, you might want to consider shutting things down and reassessing the situation. After all, you hire more team members, but doing that mid-sprint may not work. It's not easy for someone to come in mid-sprint and just hit the ground running.

Also, you might find it hard to find a qualified individual to fill the voids left by the departing members. Based on that logic, the sprint would be over, and you might not have a sound replacement. Thus, given the circumstances, it might be best to shut everything down, get new team members on board, plan the new sprint and then take it from there.

Most Scrum Masters and Product Owners try to have "backups" for team members, that is, find folks who are willing to come on to the team on short notice. While this may not always be possible, it is always good to have folks in mind who can step in a pinch hit when needed.

Another situation which may lead to the cancellation of a sprint is inadequate planning. This can lead to a poor assessment of the work that needs to be done during the Sprint Planning Meeting. For example, the Scrum team sits down to go over everything that needs to be done. The work breakdown structure is done, and the sprint gets off and running. At some point it is determined that the team will not get all the work done by the end of the sprint.

Hence, a decision needs to be made: do you begin to cut out tasks and just do what you can, or do you stop the show and go back to the drawing board?

Considering the first option, you could potentially cut out tasks as long as they don't interfere with the development of the user stories for that sprint. However, care needs to be taken in order to ensure that the cutting out tasks does not lead to an overall ineffective sprint.

The second option, and perhaps the best one, would be to just shut everything down, and go back to the drawing board. In doing this, you are ensuring that the mistakes made in planning can be corrected so that the team knows where they stand.

The problem with this solution is that it may lead to the team falling behind in schedule. Of course, this is a big deal since falling behind implies either trying to make up the work later on or having to extend the duration of the project. Either way, it's not an ideal situation.

So, what to do then?

Often, it's best to be honest and talk with the customer. Since Agile advocates for transparency, the Scrum Master can let the Product Owner know what happened and thereby have a talk with the customer about how the problems can be solved.

Many times, it is possible to make up and get the ship back on track. But it's always best to be honest and make sure that there is always a transparent solution to everything that is being done. Bear in mind that Agile is rooted in trust and communication. So, communication is vital in ensuring that everything which is done, is done in such a way that all stakeholders are on the same page.

Final thoughts

When looking at the pitfalls which may befall a Scrum team, it's important to note that these caveats can be overcome by careful planning and consideration of the circumstances which surround the project team.

At the end of the day, "team" is the operative word. When the Scrum team actually works as a team, you are able to foster positive communication and ensure that everything which is done, is done is such a way that you are being transparent and honest with all of the stakeholders in the project. You can then be transparent about setbacks and correct them.

The worst thing that you could try to do is cover up what has happened and attempt to make up for lost time later on. Sure, this might be possible when circumstances aren't as complex. Nevertheless, it is always important to keep track within the team since keeping careful track will allow everyone to be on the same page.

As such, the most important thing to keep in mind is that being focused on what needs to be done will help you maintain the discipline you need in order to guarantee your project's success. By doing exactly what needs to be done, no more and no less, you can be sure that you will meet your targets on time and with the quality your team needs to deliver. Ultimately, you want to be seen as reliable and able to deliver on the promises you make. This is what Agile and Scrum are all about.

Chapter 3: Establishing effective team mechanics

In the previous chapter, we took a close look at the pitfalls which may befall a Scrum team as a part of the development of a project. Nevertheless, it is also important to consider what can be done in order to create an effective team. As such, having adequate planning and clear guidelines is just as important as developing the proper team mechanics.

Often, Scrum practitioners are not entirely clear on how a Scrum team should actually be run. Bear in mind that Scrum teams don't run quite the same as a regular project team would. Under a traditional project management approach, the team leader or project manager would assign tasks to be done. In addition, this project lead would be in charge of supervising everyone on the team and ensure that everything gets done accordingly.

Since Agile and Scrum advocate for a flat organizational structure, it's vital that the proper team mechanics be developed in order to ensure that the team is able to work on its own and develop the discipline which is needed to get the job done with minimal supervision.

At the end of the day, that is the key, underlying factor: being able to get the job done with minimal supervision.

So, in this chapter, we will be taking a closer look at how you can develop proper team mechanics in such a way that your project will run as smoothly as possible without having to resort to micromanaging in order to get the job done.

Let's take an in-depth look at the team mechanics which will ensure your team's overall success.

Good team member traits

This is one of the most important aspects to consider when building your team.

But, what do "good team member traits" mean?

That is a fair question.

Good team member traits imply having the necessary traits that will allow team members to be effective Scrum practitioners. This implies being committed to the supporting philosophy that is espoused in Scrum.

If a team member is not fully committed to the Agile mindset, then that opens the door for team members to end up developing attitudes which are detrimental to the overall team dynamic.

For instance, if a team member wants to dominate and become the team leader. Sure, there are people with naturally dominant personalities while there are others who are much more comfortable playing a passive role within the team.

Does this mean that team members who exhibit natural leadership qualities are welcome to take over while those who are less inclined to take the lead should sit back and just do what they are told?

Hardly.

Agile advocates for team members to get equal say and participation in the development of a project. So, this implies that team members who tend to dominate should be aware that their leadership skills can be put to good use by helping those who aren't as extroverted to contribute equally.

Also, it is up to the Scrum Master to manage personalities in order to avoid having one team member boss everyone around. Solving this issue may be as simple as just reminding everyone how important it is to work collaboratively during the Daily Stand up Meeting. Other times, it may be so bad that team members may have to be replaced in order to end power struggles.

Since neither the Scrum Master nor the Product Owner are the "boss" of the project, team members must find the best way to work among themselves without having the influence of a boss telling them what to do.

That is why having qualities such as commitment and a collaborative attitude allow for successful Scrum teams. This is in addition to any technical skills which may be required in order to do the job that needs to be done as part of the project.

Here are some other qualities that Scrum team members should exhibit:

- Detail oriented
- Committed to excellence
- Strive for development

- Open-minded
- Proactive
- Service oriented

As you can see, these are mainly soft skills that Scrum team members need to exhibit throughout the course of a project in order to ensure that the work being done is actually successful. Of course, the requisite hard skills truly depend on the nature and scope of a project. As such, a software project requires a certain skill set whereas building a house requires a completely different skill set. At the end of the day, it's up to the Product Owner to understand what skills and traits are needed in order to meet the technical requirements of the project.

Self-organizing teams

Perhaps the most important team mechanic in Scrum is self-organizing teams.

This is a crucial factor that plays into Scrum. Since Scrum espouses a flat organizational structure, there is no need for an overbearing "boss" or "supervisor" who can come in and dictate what needs to be done. Sure, there are leadership roles, such as the Scrum Master, but at the end of the day, the Scrum Master does not dictate what is to be done. The decision of what should be done, and when it should be done, falls on the team as a whole.

So, during the Sprint Planning Meeting, the entire team needs to sit down and decide what will be done in that sprint, who will do what, and how it will be done. Based on that assessment, the team can get to work on the goals set forth.

In addition, it's important for the team to keep in mind that they are in charge of themselves. Therefore, this implies a greater role for personal accountability. So, if someone makes a mistake, they need to own up to it; it's not about assigning blame, but rather, it's about finding the right way to correct the mistake.

In addition, a self-organizing team must be honest about their limitations. They must be mature enough to understand when they can't do something, but also be honest about how much work can be reasonably done within the timeframe provided. What that means is that project teams should not purposely drag their feet just to make life easier for them. Bear in mind that the overarching plan is to make sure that the work that is done, is done within that reasonable time frame.

As such, allowing a team to run itself is all about empowering the team to take control and become proactive in the way they run the project. Since each sprint is planned by the Scrum team as whole, there is enough room to enable teams to base their decisions on their capabilities and limitations.

Ultimately, a self-organizing team is the epitome of collaborative work. Since everyone on the team has equal say in what is done and not done, the team is them able to make a realistic assessment of what each sprint would produce.

It is also important to keep in mind that the project team needs to have a broad idea of how long the actual project would take in order to budget the time needed in terms of the number of sprints which will be conducted. Naturally, the greater the number of sprints, the lesser the amount of work which needs to be done in each one. Ultimately, sprints can be divided in such a way that latter sprints can be used for alpha and beta testing.

These are decisions which the project team must make collectively in order to arrive at a reasonable assessment of what can and can't be done.

Transparent communication

One of the core tenets of Scrum and Agile is transparency.

Transparency is essential in enabling a clear path for the project team to carry out work in a sustainable pace while keeping project stakeholders up to speed on the project's progress. This is why keeping track of the project's progress is essential.

Transparency is also vital in determining how communication actually takes place within the group. Agile and Scrum foster an environment of trust in such a way that individuals are encouraged to be open about all aspects pertaining to the work to be done.

For instance, if a team member is having difficulty in conducting a specific task, they should be encouraged to ask for help. Often, it may boil down to the Scrum Master offering support on a technical level, or perhaps the team is lacking a specific tool which is needed in order to get the job done.

The project team may run out of a given material or may end up needing a tool they hadn't contemplated. When this happens, the team needs to be forthcoming so that the Scrum

Master can find the way to provide them with the tool, or even information, that the project team needs.

Also, transparent communication happens between the project team and the customer. Both the project team and the customer need to be on the same page regarding the work that is being done and the progress being made. So, transparency in communication is intended to discourage the customer from springing up additional requests without considering the project team's capabilities.

In addition, the project team needs to be forthcoming with the customer if they happen to encounter a difficulty which may delay the final release of the project's outputs. If this should be the case, the project team needs to be clear about how the situation can be remedied and how they can deliver, within a reasonable time frame, on the final release of the project.

Then, there's the topic of cost. If the project should overrun in cost, for whatever reason, the project team must be clear and honest about why the project has overrun its initial cost expectations and how that can be managed in such a way that the customer is clear about why the costs have exceeded initial projections.

If such cost overruns are due to additional customer requests, then it is easier to have the customer see the reasoning behind the additional cost. But if the cost overrun is due to some issue encountered by the project team, especially if it was an unforeseen issue, then the customer needs to be aware of it. However, cost overruns may not be absorbed by the customer, but rather, may be shared among the customer and team, or in the worst of cases, absorbed by the team especially if it is the team's responsibility.

Consequently, the ultimate goal of transparent communication is to ensure that all stakeholders in the project have a clear understanding of what is to be done, and where each party stands.

Cross functionality

One of the most important aspects of a Scrum team is cross functionality.

In short, cross functionality refers to being able to carry out different functions across the entire team. That implies that each team member would be able to do the same functions as the next member. While this may seem like overlap, it is quite useful particularly when you are considering the importance of having various team members support each other.

As such, cross functional teams are able to back each other up at all times especially when there is one team member that may be lacking expertise in a given area. Also, there are circumstances in which one team member has a specific skill set which is ideal for a given task.

In that regard, the entire team may rally around that individual and complete the required tasks. In addition, having strong team members in different areas will facilitate the work being done especially when other team members may be lacking that expertise.

Ultimately, a cross functional team is about utilizing everyone's talents and expertise in such a way that every team member is a valued contributor. Consequently, every team member is on the team because they have unique contributions to make which enhance the team's overall ability to perform and deliver on the project's objectives.

For instance, you may have a group of engineers. Since they are all engineers, they all share the same common training in the basics of engineering. But since they all have different specialties, they are able to support each other.

So, you would have one engineer whose expertise is in structures, another whose expertise is in electrical, and so on.

The sum of this project team will allow them to design and construct a building without having overlapping functions and utilizing each of their individual skill sets. At the end of the day, this is the best combination of abilities and talents which you could hope for.

The right size of teams

One of the most common questions regarding Scrum is what the right size for a team should be.

The answer to this question depends on the scale and size of the project. To most outside observers, Scrum is seen as a limited proposition in which Scrum methodology can only accommodate one Scrum team per project. While we will be getting into scaling Scrum a bit later on, it is worth mentioning at this point that Scrum provides ample opportunity for scalability at much broader levels.

So, whether it is one Scrum team working on an individual project, or whether it is a group of Scrum teams working together on one larger project, each, individual Scrum squad does have a recommended size.

In essence, each Scrum squad should range somewhere between 4 to 8 members. Ideally, Scrum teams would have even numbers in order to accommodate for sectioning off a Scrum team into pairs if need be. This is an important consideration as Scrum advocates for collaborative work. Consequently, having odd-numbered teams would make it a bit more complex to section off work.

Also, having odd-numbered teams may end up promoting individual work since there is always one team member that would not have a pair. While it is not required for Scrum teams to work in pairs, it is a good idea for Scrum teams to encourage pair work. This is just another way in which Scrum teams can foster collaborative work.

Given the fact that 4 to 8 members is a good range, practice has shown that a good number is 6 members per team. This number of members would allow for the creation of 3, 2-member squads, while still having a manageable number of overall members. Another useful configuration of a 6-member team would be 2, 3-member squads.

The recommended minimum should be 4 members because 3 members may be too few members especially if a member leaves mid-way through a sprint. That would leave two members on the team, and of course, that may not be enough manpower to get through a sprint successfully.

If a team should have more than 8 members, the group a whole may be too large for a single Scrum Master to support. If a Scrum team needs to have more than 8 members, the Product Owner may consider having two Development Teams set, each with its own Scrum Master.

Of course, it is not as simple as just dividing up teams and getting additional Scrum Masters. There is a logistic constraint that would affect this proposition considering the fact that budgetary limitations may not allow for the hiring of additional team members or additional Scrum Masters. However, if the scope of a project is truly broad, then multiple Scrum teams may be the best way to go.

As such, 6 members seems to be the right size for a Scrum team as based on experience. It provides flexibility for the Scrum team, while providing a manageable team size that can work closely together and allow the Scrum Master a good, individualized attention scheme. Furthermore, 6-member teams can absorb the loss of a member much better than a 4-member team could. Teams greater than 8 members may also lead to a breakdown in the collaborative nature of the project as it fosters for subgroups to be formed within the larger project team.

Focus on commitment

An important trait that individuals need to share is commitment. For the team, as a whole, commitment means keeping a concerted, unified team effort in which the entire team can maintain a steady tempo.

Commitment also refers to ensuring that team members work in unison. Working in unison means knowing what everyone else is working on and also letting others know what you are working on. Ultimately, this boils down to transparency. Within a committed team, transparency opens the door to generate committed teams whose sole purpose is to further the accomplishment of the mission objectives set forth in the project.

In essence, the Scrum Master, as the coordinator of activities, needs to act as a type of "cheerleader" in such a way that individual team members are focused and committed on achieving the project's deliverables.

One important consideration on commitment is that the required traits for individual team members must be made aware of what is expected of them in terms of how they fit in the team as a whole. Consequently, individual team members who do not share the overall vision of the team may end up becoming a hindrance to the team's overall purpose.

Finally, it is imperative that the Scrum Master be a good role model in terms of their commitment to the team. In that regard, the Scrum Master leads by example so that the team, as a whole, can gain a deeper feeling of belonging and commitment. As the Scrum Master exhibits a committed attitude toward their team, the team will gain a greater sense of working together toward a common purpose in achieving the ultimate project aims.

Commitment is also a state of mind. Within the Agile mindset, commitment is all about delivering value to the customer and the end users of the final deliverables. As reflected in the Agile manifesto, delivering value to customers is the most important objective that Scrum pursues in every project. As such, this mindset is the ideal state under which a Scrum team should focus their efforts.

It is also worth noting that commitment is all about making sure that there is shared vision among all of the members of a project team. By having a shared vision, the project team can be sure that each task that needs to be completed is done in accordance to the overarching goals set at the beginning of each sprint.

So, it certainly pays to take the time to make sure that everyone is on the same page and working toward the same target.

Keeping a sustainable pace

One of the most important aspects of project management, in general, is maintaining sustainable pace in the development of a project. When you are unable to maintain a sustainable pace, you are setting yourself up for failure.

As such, it's important to note that it is vital for both a Scrum Master and Development Team to understand how long it realistically takes to get the job done. This is vital since an underestimation of time needed to complete a task could potentially become disastrous to the overall completion of the plan.

The best way to assess how long a task will take to complete is experience. Experience is the best way to determine how long a project will realistically take. However, there are cases when a project is completely new. In such cases, it may be hard to determine how long a project will actually take. Under these circumstances, it's important to overestimate the time that a project would take in order to complete a project. At the end of the day, it's worth buying your team more time. If you do have time leftover, you can always use this time to conduct testing.

Also, care needs to be taken in order to avoid sprinting out of the gate and running out of steam mid-way through the project. This type of mistake can easily be made when you are eager to get as much done is as brief a period of time as possible.

The main drawback with attempting to keep an unsustainable pace is that you run the risk of burning the team out. Of course, there may be times in which it is necessary to take things up a notch. But that can be a temporary situation especially when unforeseen issues come up. But this should only be a temporary approach.

In the long run, it's best for the Scrum Master to sit down with their team and work on a plan that will ensure a realistic tempo. For instance, it might be that one particular Scrum team is comfortable with working 10 or 12 hours a day. That might not be the norm, but it is not unheard of. Similarly, it could be that the Scrum team is rather inexperienced and might be more inclined to working an 8-hour day.

In the end, it's up to the Scrum Master to see how comfortable the team might be with working a certain number of hours and what the limits of that might be. Experienced Scrum Masters will have a intuitive feel for the way a Scrum team will be able to work based on the parameters of a given project. The main thing to keep in mind is that the overall tempo of a project should be dictated by the team and not by the Scrum Master. This will ensure the successful completion of the project within the schedule, and budget, that was intended.

Tolerance to failure

When we discussed the possibility of cancelling a sprint, the concept of failure was right in the middle of it. In essence, failure boiled down to being unable to complete the objectives set forth at the outset of the sprint. While the inability to complete objectives may not be the direct fault of the Scrum team, the end result does fall on the shoulders of the Scrum team.

As such, what can be done?

How can failure to achieve a task be dealt with?

The fact of the matter is that failure is nothing more than a learning experience. It is an opportunity to grow as a team and move on. Failure allows individual team members to learn from their experience and achieve a greater understanding of the way Scrum works and the way that the project-related tasks can be completed.

Now, failure is a positive so long as we're not talking about complete breakdown and failure to continue with the project. While cancelling a sprint may not be the end of the world, it should also be noted that we are not talking about shutting the entire project down.

On a deeper level, failure is a way of assessing the way a team is working. Under this assessment, the reasons for the failure can be determined and corrective measures may emerge from it. Perhaps the reason for the failure was a lack of expertise in one area, or perhaps it was due to inappropriate planning. Whatever the reason, the Scrum Master needs to sit down with their team and determine where things went wrong and what needs to be done in order to avoid it happening again.

Nevertheless, a line needs to be drawn at some point.

While learning failure leads to meaningful learning experiences, there is a point in which failure cannot be tolerated any further. It is at this point in which the Scrum Master, and a larger extent the Product Owner, need to make it clear that failure to deliver is unacceptable.

A good rule of thumb in this case is that failure should not be tolerated when it jeopardizes the completing of a sprint. Such failure may even doom the entire project's completion. As such, there should be no room for tolerance of such types of failure.

Again, there could be unforeseen issues which go beyond the control of the team. That much is clear. But if failure stems from negligence or just inadequate planning, then measure needs to be put into place in order to avoid further instances of such failure.

Ultimately, the best antidote to failure is conscious planning and commitment. By ensuring that planning is realistic and based on sound fundamentals, while having a committed team on board, then the chances of failure are greatly reduced.

Building a culture of feedback and continuous improvement

The final point in this chapter pertains to the importance of feedback.

Feedback is a crucial factor which can facilitate the achievement of project aims. Scrum teams should not be afraid of feedback. After all, negative feedback should be seen as a growth opportunity much the same way failure can be transformed into a positive outcome.

However, most individuals are afraid of feedback for fear of being judged in a negative light. But if things are going as well as they should, it is a great opportunity for all of the team members in involved to take a long look at one another and determine where things have gone wrong and where things can be improved.

Feedback, for better or for worse, can lead to continuous improvement.

If a team believes that everything it does is perfect, then they really are doing themselves a disservice. When you believe that everything you do is as good as it's going to get, then you are committed. You are not committed to improving and you are not committed to making the best of your opportunities to become better at what you do.

When you take feedback for what it is, it provides you with the opportunity to build on your current knowledge and experience. That can lead to improved performance in future projects down the road. Since you cannot expect to be perfect, you can always expect to improve upon your previous experiences.

How can you embrace a culture of feedback?

By being transparent and forthcoming.

There should be no need to be afraid of feedback if you are committed to doing things the best way you can and are committed to improving. That's it. That's all it takes.

Unless you are closed to improving upon your skills and your ability to continuously grow, then feedback can become an important ally for your team. Embrace the feedback received from customers; embrace the feedback received from peers, and certainly embrace the feedback which you can get from within your own team. The feedback that your own team can produce as a result of a self-assessment can go a long toward building a culture of excellence on all levels.

So, look at feedback as a valuable tool for your team's improvement and development. The Sprint Retrospective Meetings can be used to critique the work done in the previous sprint and how any shortcomings can be improved. And if there aren't any shortcomings to consider, then encourage your team to value new ways of doing things. You never know when you might come across a breakthrough. Such breakthroughs can lead to significant impacts on the same project, or future projects.

Chapter 4: Building a high-performance team

Scrum is all about high performance.

If your team does not perform at its best, then something is lacking. What this implies is that your team is not fully taking advantage of its skills and expertise.

Now, a high-performance team does not mean that you are furiously working long hours on end and producing massive amounts of results. A high-performance team is about producing the right results within the time and budget you determined at the outset of your project.

As we have highlighted throughout this book, building a great Scrum team is all about setting up the right culture among the team. If you are able to harness this culture, then you will be able to build a successful team around solid values and virtues.

At this point, it's worth underscoring the fact that the building of a strong team shouldn't be about finding a magic formula which can be used to produce results overnight. Rather, the right formula in this case is about building a culture from within which fosters development, creativity and an overall sense of purpose for your team.

When you are able to create this greater sense of belonging and commitment in your team, you are able to fulfill the expectations of your team at all levels. By fostering the feelings of commitment and belonging, you will be able to ensure that your team will be focused on getting the best possible results within the most reasonable terms.

Setting the right culture for creativity and collaboration

Setting up a good team culture is about setting up the Scrum team for success. When you are able to set up your team for success, you will be able to get the results you are looking for without having to sacrifice the individuality of each team member. This is important since every individual is capable of producing results and getting the most out of the opportunity they have to participate on the team.

Think of sports teams.

In team sports, positions are generally well-defined. That means that the players on the team have a clear idea of what they are meant to do and what they are expected to produce. When players don't have a clear idea of the position they are meant to play, then the results will speak for themselves. The players which have a keen understanding of the position they play and their role on the team are generally able to produce much better results. The reason for this is that they will not do anything that is not asked of them. Instead, they will do exactly what is expected of them. This implies that this clear understanding of their role gives them focus and purpose.

Also, you will hear about players being out of their natural position. What that means is that a player may be in a position which does not suit their individual talents and abilities. So, it's up to the coach to find the best way to get that player back into their natural role. By having a player outside of their natural role, the player is not being set up for success.

The same thing happens in any project environment. If the team member is not in a position in which they are comfortable and experienced, then they are setting themselves up for failure. Ultimately, this is not the type of failure which is conducive to learning. Rather, this is the type of learning which is conducive to destroying team morale and motivation.

This is where a Scrum Master must be a good judge of character and come up with the best way in which they can recognize when a team member is out of their element and in which cases a team member simply needs a nudge in the right direction.

With that in mind, Scrum Masters need to become familiar with the right ways in which they can motivate their team to constantly perform to the best of their capabilities. As such, we will be taking a look at an effective way in which a Scrum team can be effective and produce high-octane results on a consistent basis.

Using workshops to set the values for teams

At the outset of any project, a good Scrum Master will bring their team in for a meeting to plan out the work to be conducted throughout the entire project as divided up in each sprint and the subsequent work breakdown for each sprint.

This initial meeting is a great opportunity for setting up the ground rules of the project especially when team members are new to each other, that is, when team members are not familiar with one another. So, the Scrum Master has the opportunity to make things work in such a way that the entire team is on the same page from day one.

The ideal means of achieving this is through a workshop.

This workshop can be planned by both the Scrum Master and Product Owner, but ideally delivered by the Scrum Master. Now, it could be one workshop, or perhaps a series of workshops in which the team is familiar with what is expected of them and what they are expected to produce.

So, a good workshop should be oriented at providing a Scrum team with the foundation needed in order to perform at a high level.

Of course, all team members should be familiar with Scrum and Agile, and preferably certified to some extent in Scrum methodology. If a Scrum Master intends to use Scrum as the project methodology with a team that is unfamiliar with Scrum or has never worked with Scrum before, then a single workshop may not be enough to get everyone on board.

This workshop is intended to bring individuals, who are familiar with Scrum, together in a single environment so that they can work together toward a single end result.

The main objective of a pre-project workshop should be to establish the team's values. These values should be geared toward the successful completion of the project. It's that simple. If there are team members who are looking out for themselves and are reticent about working collaboratively, then finding a replacement for them before the project starts is the ideal time to do so.

When conducting a pre-project workshop, the Scrum Master should be looking to harmonize every individual's personal beliefs and attitudes so that the team can work toward the common goal of delivering value to the customer, early and often.

So, what would such a workshop look like?

Let's consider the following example.

Joe is a Scrum Master who has recently assembled a team of six members. The customer has hired the Scrum team to produce a marketing campaign for a new product launch. So, the Scrum team is made up of graphic designers, marketing experts, social media managers and a statistician.

Since the team members are new to the team, each member is unfamiliar with one another. So, there is a clear need to harmonize the team's efforts and direction in order to find a good rhythm for the team to perform. This is important since the fact that each member is unfamiliar with one another can lead to a steep learning curve.

So, the Scrum Master has assembled the team and taken some time to sit down with the team, as a whole, and go over what the project is about and what the final outcomes should be. But then, the next issue becomes: how to take a group of individuals and get them to become a cohesive unit that is dedicated to achieving a specific outcome?

That's where the magic of a good workshop comes into play.

At the outset of a project, the Scrum Master can bring his team in together for the initial project planning meeting.

During this meeting, the Scrum team meets for the first time. As such, it is very important to break the ice particularly if the team members are not familiar with one another. So, breaking the ice can be something as simple as having team members introduce themselves and talk about their experience. But this is only scratching the surface.

One of the mayor objectives of this project planning meeting should be to come away with a "playbook" of sorts. This playbook is intended to be the major guidelines for what the team is expected to do and how they plan to achieve it. Thus, the playbook can be a collection of techniques and strategies which can be used to achieve the project outcomes.

In our example, Joe has assembled a team of marketing experts who are familiar with the way a successful marketing campaign can be put together. So, the team has assembled to go over the major tasks that will be conducted throughout the life of the project. Also, they will discuss an estimation as to the overall amount of time the project will take.

Once the team has determined the major tasks that will be conducted and a general estimation of the overall time the entire project will take, the Scrum team can then move on to brainstorm ideas and ways in which each of the tasks can be completed. Also, the Scrum team can decide who will be responsible for each task.

This can lead to a very general work breakdown structure in which the main tasks to be covered in each sprint can be determined. This, in turn, leads to techniques and strategies being matched up with tasks to be conducted and the team member responsible for it. Consequently, the team is ready to get down to work and get things done.

So, what are the outcomes of this initial meeting?

1. The team is aware of each member's strengths and experience
2. The main tasks which need to be completed (there may or may not be user stories at this point, but just a general idea of what needs to be done in order to meet the customer's requirements)

3.   A rough estimate of how long it will take to get it done (unless the customer has fixed a specific amount of time)
4.   The number of sprints which may be required
5.   Who will be responsible for each task
6.   Techniques and strategies that can be utilized to achieve the main tasks

At this point, there are no specifics determined yet as this initial phase is intended to produce the main outline of what is expected to be produced at the end of the project. Most importantly, each team member already has an idea of how they will approach each task.

So, when the first Sprint Planning Meeting rolls around, each team member will know where they fit into the project and how they can approach the work that needs to be done in that initial sprint. This is especially important if team members are working with each other for the first time.

Consequently, having a clear idea of how the first sprint is going to be planned with allow the Scrum team to come up with a good way of approaching the work that needs to be done and what potential requirements may come about from needing to get this work done.

One final point about this initial project meeting: Scrum does not advocate for extensive documentation. So, how can you go about recording the topics discussed at this meeting without generating too much documentation?

The simplest way of recording all of this information is through a good, old-fashioned spreadsheet.

On a spreadsheet, the information discussed can be captured and distributed among team members is a format which is easy to read and easy to edit.

It may look something like this:

Task	Sprint	Strategies	Assigned to
Conduct customer survey	Sprint two	Skype calls, face-to-face meetings, phone interviews	Joe

As you can see from this example, tracking your team's progress doesn't have to be hard or complex. It can be solved by means of a simple spreadsheet focused on keeping score of what is agreed upon by all team members. And, of course, it is not set in stone meaning that it can be altered and modified as circumstances dictate. It could be that once you reach the Sprint Planning Meeting, the team realizes that someone else is more qualified than Joe to carry out this task. Or, it might be that the team has decided that this particular task is not needed in the project at all. Furthermore, the team may have decided that this task needs to be broken up into smaller tasks and so on.

Whatever ends up being decided at the initial planning stages of the project serves as a guide for what will be covered in each, individual sprint. But it's not until the team actually sit down to plan each, individual sprint, that the plans are finalized.

Nevertheless, the team is already clear on where it wants to go by the time it reaches the Sprint Planning Meeting. This provides clarity and a sense of direction for both the Scrum Master and the Development Team in order for them to gain a clear understanding of how the project's work breakdown structure will ultimately look like.

Determining what is important to your team

In the previous example pertaining to the workshop at the outset of the project, the team sat down and worked out what were the priority areas for the project. This means that the broad strokes of the work to be done were determined in addition to the main aspects to be addressed.

However, it is also up to the team to decide what is really important to them.

What does it mean to determine what is really important to them?

Well, think about it this way: the project team, while focused on delivering value to the customer, is focused on finding a new way of doing something which has already been tried and tested. This has become important to the Scrum team since they are eager to innovate and make a significant change in a rather traditional area.

While this may be an ambitious approach, the Scrum team feels that if they seek to innovate something which has been traditionally done in a certain way, they will be able to make a significant impact moving forward.

Such an approach can be underscored by something such as incorporating a new technology in something that has been traditionally done by hand. Or, it could be a new technology which supersedes a previous one. Perhaps the project team is eager to apply a new methodology that challenges the results of previous versions of the same methodology.

In this case, the Scrum team is committed to delivering value to the customer as usual, but the team has also determined that it is of value to them to try a new approach in the development of the new project deliverables. This implies that the team is also very eager to innovate.

In other cases, the Scrum team might be more concerned about getting the job done as fast as they can in order to have more time for testing. In this approach, the team has determined that testing is important to them since previous experience has shown them that a lack of testing led to a series of bugs once the product was released.

Ultimately, the project team needs to decide what they really want to get out of the project. And, they are free to do so as long as what they are aiming for is something that will contribute to the overall success of the project. It would make no sense for the project team to focus on aspects and areas which have no bearing on the overall completion of the project. For instance, the project team is more concerned about setting up a comfortable workspace rather than getting the job done itself. Such attitudes would lead to the project team becoming bogged down by unimportant details.

Using metrics to measure the product and the team

Metrics, and thereby measuring, are fundamental aspects of any project. When you set out on a project, your focus should be on quantifying the performance of the team and the effectiveness of the product being developed.

When the product is under development, testing can be done in order to determine if the product is living up to standards. In such cases, problems and bugs can be caught during testing, fixed and then provide a quality product.

As such, it's rather straightforward on how to measure the effectiveness of a product.

What is not so straightforward is how to measure the effectiveness of the Scrum team.

In this aspect, it might get a bit tricky as to how to measure the overall effectiveness of the team. You might consider the following criteria to measure team effectiveness and performance:

- Number of user stories completed
- Tasks completed
- Incomplete/failed tasks
- Team turnover
- Number of bugs found
- Defects per parts
- Feedback

These are some examples of criteria which can be used to measure overall team performance.

For instance, the project contemplates a certain amount of user stories as reflected by the project itself. So, one sprint may include the completion of three user stories. However, the Development Team was only able to complete two.

In this case, the criteria indicate that the team had a subpar performance since they were unable to complete all three of the user stories planned for that sprint.

Of course, the question then becomes: why was the Development Team unable to complete all three user stories?

It could be that they ran out of time, there were unforeseen issues, team members left the project, and so on. Whatever the reason, the Scrum Master and even the Product Owner must determine what went wrong in order to correct it.

Also, the Development Team could be measured by the number of assigned tasks completed. If the Development Team is able to complete all of the tasks assigned to that individual sprint, then there is no doubt the sprint was successful. However, if there were incomplete tasks, then it boils down to determining which tasks were left incomplete and why.

Furthermore, the project team may be measured by the overall turnover in project staff. For instance, the team started off with 6 team members. By the end of the first sprint, two members had to be replaced. By the end of the second sprint, another two members had left, and so on. Perhaps it's just the one position that has constant turnover. Consequently, the Scrum Master needs to figure out why that specific position keeps generating turnover.

Now, if the project team should have zero turnover, then it might be considered a reflection on how well the team is run. In any event, the important thing to bear in mind is that the project team is able to complete the tasks that are assigned to them within the allotted period of time.

Notwithstanding, there is a certain level of quality which must be met by the Development Team in order to determine that the project has been successful. For instance, the project team may "complete" all of their assigned tasks, but the output is of such bad quality, that it is not functional as per specifications.

This also leads to the concept of defects per parts. This approach is typical to manufacturing in which quality is measure by the number of defects in a given amount of production. For example, you may have defects measured in parts per million, or perhaps in lines of code, or better yet, in each instance a service is provided.

And then there is feedback. This could be one of the most significant criteria used to measure a team's effectiveness. If the criteria show that a team was ineffective as perceived by the customer based on the final output, then that criteria can be used to determine the team was ineffective. If, on the contrary, the customer is thrilled with the final outcome of the product, then the team would be considered a success.

In much the same way a team's performance can be measured, so can the overall effectiveness of the final product. Its effectiveness can be measured in the way the product is able to solve the user stories or meet the customer's expectations.

So, you could have a product which meets all of the technical criteria, but that doesn't solve the actual needs of the customer. Or, you could have a fabulous product which checks off all the boxes and delivers the value the customer expects. This would mean that both the team and product have been successful.

Using a dashboard to track metrics

Determining which metrics to use in order to track progress is only the first step. The next step is to determine how to keep track of those metrics and also how to display them. That is where a dashboard comes in handy.

A dashboard can be as a simple as having a spreadsheet that tracks data and then displaying the final totals at the bottom of the page. This would enable the Scrum team to see the sum of the data and determine if it is producing what is expected.

Of course, dashboards can be far more complex. You might want to use gauges to visually represent the metrics that are being tracked much the same way a dashboard is outfitted in a car.

The main reason for using a dashboard is to have a visual representation of where the progress of the team, and the final product, are headed. This will enable all interested parties to see how things are coming along. As such, it ties into transparency and being forthcoming about everything that goes on in the project.

Best of all, by having a clear measure of the performance of a project, errors and efficient performance can be corrected ahead of time and in a clear and concise fashion. So, all team members can be on the same page and make the most of the important information which is displayed to the on the dashboard.

One very important note, updating the dashboard is just as important as updating the Scrum board. While the Scrum board specifically tracks the tasks that are completed and in progress, the dashboard tracks other data the project team considers important. Consequently, the lack of updates to the dashboard may result in having an incomplete picture of what is truly going on. So, it pays to make sure that the project data is being updated accordingly. This will enable all team members to be on the same page and allow the customer to be informed about where the project is headed.

Final thoughts

Building a high-performance team is no easy task. But the main point to keep in mind is that building a high-performance team is vital to ensuring the project's outcomes. Thus, when the project deliverables are presented, all stakeholders in the project can be sure that such outcomes will meet their expectations.

By following the strategies outlined in this chapter, you can lay the groundwork for building a successful team that will be committed with the completion of the project and delivering the greatest amount of value that can possible be delivered.

This leads to a sustainable pace and committed attitude as the fruits of the Development Team's efforts become evident to the customer and to all stakeholders in the project. This is the reason why having up to date information is part of being transparent and honest. There is no need to hide information from anyone. But at the same time, it is also important that the data collection be congruent with the reality that the project team is actually living.

So, when your team sets out on a new project, your understanding of what your team expects and what they value will help you build a successful team that will win every time. All you have to do is know exactly what to look for in each player and make sure they are in the right spot on the team.

Chapter 5: Getting everyone on board... and keeping them there

Thus far, we have talked about getting the right people on board and getting them on the same shared vision. We have had an in-depth discussion on all of these aspects throughout this book. But, believe it or not, we still have lots more to discuss.

You see, building the right team isn't just about magically finding the right staff. It's about really knowing what you are looking for and going down that road. After all, not all personalities are the same and not all folks would be able to gel on the same team. That's a fundamental point since having talented individuals, but who don't really get along, may be a detrimental for the team as having folks who have no clue about what they are doing.

So, there must be a happy medium right?

In fact, there is. That is why we are having this discussion in this chapter. Throughout this book, we have discussed how important it is to get a shared vision which is conducive to building the right team culture and enabling the entire team to become successful on a large scale. However, we haven't touched upon how to actually assemble the right team members.

Often, it is not easy for Scrum Masters and Product Owners to find the right team members. After all, the core of any successful Scrum-based project is to find the right people which can comprise the team and thereby make a successful Scrum team.

But, where can you find these folks?

Most importantly, how can you determine if they are the right folks for the job?

These are questions which you can answer by taking a deeper look at your project's vision and philosophy.

On the surface, we have discussed the main traits that team members ought to exhibit, such as, being open minded, committed and detail oriented. Nevertheless, how can you determine if a given individual stacks up accordingly?

You can usually tell if a potential team member is right for your team if they are willing to buy into your project's vision. When you develop this vision, you can then "sell" it to potential team members. The more they buy into the vision and underlying philosophy, the easier it will be for you to attract the right team members.

You can build your project's vision and philosophy by using a structured approach such as the "Product Canvas."

The Product Canvas is just that, a canvas, which displays the main aspects of the project in a visual format which can enable any observer to get a clear picture of where the project is going, what it is about, and what needs to get done.

Many times, Product Owners and Scrum Masters have trouble getting their vision for the project across because they are unable to truly articulate their thoughts. By utilizing a graphic organizer, it is a lot easier for potential team members to make a clear assessment if they can deliver, or not, on this project.

The Product Canvas has the following sections:

1. The goal
2. The metrics
3. The target group
4. The big picture
5. The product details

These are the components of the Product Canvas. When you are able to put all of these aspects together, you are able to create a holistic vision for your final product which can be easily articulated and transmitted to the project team, or any outside observer. This is especially important if you are seeking outside sources of funding for your project, or if there are addition project stakeholders that you need to bring on board.

That being said, the Product Canvas acts as a dashboard that can be permanently displayed and consistently used as a reference for the duration of the project.

Now, let's discuss each of these items in greater detail.

- **The goal**. This is the main objective of the project. In short, it is what you are trying to achieve with the final outcome of your project. This could realistically be anything that you are striving to achieve. For instance, it could be to boost sales, increase the number of subscribers, or just introducing a brand into the market. Whatever the objective, it must be a clear depiction of the reason for creating the final product.

- **The metrics**. These metrics do not pertain to the development of the final product, but rather to the performance of the final product. For instance, if your goal were to create an app which will increase the number of subscribers to your company's service, then the clearest metric would be the number of new subscribers your app has generated. Let's say that you are looking to increase the amount of sales, then your metric would be the actual dollar figures attached to those sales via the use of the app.

- **The target group**. This one is fairly straightforward. This section refers to the end users of the final product you are creating. These users are represented by the user stories you have created for the final version of the product.

- **The big picture.** This aspect refers to the process that it will take to reach the final outcome you have set for your project. This refers to the actual design process, the development of the final deliverables and how the final product will be tracked in order to determine if the project's overall scope has been successful. With this, you can keep a constant track of where the lifecycle of the project is heading.

- **The product details**. These items will serve as a tie-in for the following stages of the product's development. As such, this will enable you to see where the next steps lie in the product. For instance, you could be looking at tracking specific product features to see how they impact the overall performance of the of final deliverables. You may end up finding out that the features which you thought would generate the most impact did not while other seemingly less important features were the ones that generated the greatest amount of impact.

As you can see, the Product Canvas is a rather complete approach which you can use to make the most out of your product planning and get your project's objectives of the group. The main thing to bear in mind is that the end user, that is the customer that will actually benefit from the outcomes of this project, should be at the forefront of the efforts intended in the project's development. Furthermore, the project team needs to be aware that the customer who is behind the project itself, in addition to other project stakeholders, needs to be put at the forefront of the development stages. Hence, the Development Team truly finds itself in at the service of those for whom the project is intended.

Creating a Scrum team

The development of the Product Canvas is a great start to the project. In fact, it is highly recommended to have this canvas set up prior to the hiring of Development Team members. The reason for this is that when a potential member is considered for the team, they will know exactly what is expected of them and what they need to do in order to meet the objectives of the project.

As such, the Product Canvas can either be developed by the Product Owner, or by the

Product Owner and the Scrum Master in tandem. I have also pointed out that the Scrum Master may choose to develop this canvas with the Development Team especially in those cases where the project's outcomes have not been developed before. Thus, the Development Team may have the required skills and tools that the Scrum Master and the Product Owner may lack.

In such cases, it would be recommended that the Product Canvas be developed with an experienced team that has either worked together before or has had some exposure to Scrum and Agile. When the Development Team are experienced, it is easier to avoid setbacks since the team knows where it is going and has a better understanding for what the Agile and Scrum worlds will require of them.

Assuming that the Scrum Master, or Product Owner, has already developed the canvas, then they can go out to find the right members for the team. Getting these team members on board boils down to finding the folks with the right attitude, the right skill set and of course, who agree with the compensation package attached to their participation in the project.

Compensation of team members is always a sticky subject.

After all, how can you determine how much a team member should earn?

That depends on a number of variables, such as, your budget. Also, it might boil down to your ability, or lack thereof, of procuring enough funds to even pay the Development Team a competitive wage. This is where having people buy into your project's philosophy becomes one of the most important aspects of the project's vision.

Therefore, Development Team members have to be committed with the project's vision especially if their initial compensation may not be as attractive as expected. Your project's compensation structure may be tied to the overall product's success. So, if the final product is successful, the team gets paid. If it fails, then the team essentially works for nothing,

An "all or nothing" approach may be a bit too much for some folks to stomach. So, they may not buy into the project's vision. But you may find folks who are willing to give their time and efforts in building a project which won't pay off in the short run but has the potential to pay off considerably in the long run. These folks may be driven to build something worthwhile which would ultimately lead the to gaining far more than if they had gotten paid for the work up front.

Determining the right members

Consequently, the right team members are those who are committed to the project's vision. It should be said that if you are hiring employees to go along with the work that needs to be done in order to produce your project's final outcomes, then you will get employees.

What does that mean?

It means that employees will do what they do in exchange for a salary. They won't be committed to producing the right outcome. They will only be concerned with doing the bare minimum in order to get the job done and collect their pay. That's it. They won't be committed with doing their best. While they may be committed to learn and gain experience, employees won't give their all for the sake of the project.

So, the right team members are those who are personally committed with the outcomes. It could be that it boils down to a personal commitment with the other individual team members. It might be that this project offers an individual to work on something they have always wanted to work on. Or, it might even allow a team member the opportunity to prove to themselves, and thereby everyone else, that they are capable of working at a given level.

So, these various motivations are important for you to understand when assembling your team. If you are looking for employees, then you will get folks who are in it for the money. Plain and simple. But if you are looking for folks who are truly motivated and will have a personal interest in making their contributions really count, then your project must give them the opportunity to shine, especially if they haven't had the opportunity to do so before.

Ultimately, your team should be able to offer everyone the opportunity to contribute equally in such a way that all team members are partners. This is the reason for the flat structure. If you allow individual members to feel like employees, then you are opening the door for team members to feel undervalued and underappreciated. At the end of the day, this will kill your team's motivation and drive.

How to select the right members

Once you have figured out the opportunities that your project has to offer, you can use that as a "sales pitch." This pitch isn't about offering people opportunities for growth and learning in lieu of payment. Sure, if you can afford to pay people so that they can pay their bills, then do so. They will appreciate the income. But if beyond the income there are opportunities to grow and develop skills which are useful to them, then you have a valuable proposition for individual team members.

By the same token, you also need to have a clear checklist of what you are looking for. That checklist may include the hard and soft skills that are required for the successful completion of your project. After all, you might have committed individuals but who lack the technical knowledge needed in order to carry out the project itself. Therefore, you would have to make a choice, would this team member's lack of experience of technical know-how be offset by their attitude.

Consider this situation.

You are looking for engineers to work on a construction project. As such, you are looking for individuals who are committed to building the structure, but who would have to be willing to accept a lower than market compensation structure.

Consequently, this compensation structure may attract younger, less experienced engineers who are looking to get their feet wet in the business. As such, are you willing to accept less-experienced engineers who are looking to gain experience?

If you find that you cannot afford to have less experienced staff, then you might have to up your compensation structure in order to attract more experience and knowledgeable engineers. But if you feel comfortable with that type of on-the-job-training situation, then you could perfectly consider hiring less experienced engineers, but who have a solid technical background as learned in college.

Now, I will say this: often having less experienced people on a project may lead to greater innovation. The rationale behind this statement is that it is often seen that more experienced folks tend to have a way of doing things. Therefore, if a team member is set in their ways, then Agile may seem a bit extreme for them. Thus, your project team may not fully embrace change and innovation as well as you hope they would.

At the end of the day, the selection of the right team members boils down to the personalities which would mesh the best with the overall philosophy and scope of the project. If you find that folks are approaching your team because they are hoping to get paid, then you might have to find other folks who might be less concerned about money (even though they would need the paycheck), but who are more concerned about gaining experience and making the most of their opportunity to participate in a project such as yours.

Selecting the right Scrum Master

The choice of a Scrum Master is just as critical as that of the individual team members.

If your choice for Scrum Master is a "boss," then you might be in trouble. The Scrum Master is not anyone's boss. In fact, under the Scrum umbrella, there are no bosses. There are just team members working together toward a common goal. That's all.

If your perception of a Scrum Master is all-knowing, fearless leader, then you might have the wrong vision in mind.

A Scrum Master is, by definition, a subservient leader. This means that as a project leader, the Scrum Master puts their team ahead of themselves. This is a crucial aspect to a Scrum Master. If your choice for a Scrum Master is not willing to put the team ahead of themselves, you might be setting your team up for an unpleasant situation.

Now, having such a person is not necessarily a bad thing; it's just that that is not the Agile mindset. Having such a personality "running" things might be better suited for a more traditional project management approach, in which case, you might consider a different project management approach.

Also, the Scrum Master should be someone who is knowledgeable and understands the way Scrum and Agile work, but who is also knowledgeable in the way the actual product works.

Consider this: you know of a very experienced Scrum Master. This person has ample experience in software development but hasn't worked on marketing projects before. So, you can't be sure that this Scrum Master's experience will translate into a successful marketing campaign. There is a chance that it would, but odds are it may not.

So, this is why selecting the right Scrum Master, with the right profile, may prove to be the hardest task of all. Your choice of a Scrum Master will ultimately boil down to finding a committed individual, who is happy with the compensation structure, and is able to check their ego at the door.

This is just like sports.

The best team players are the most talented individuals who are also willing to play as a team and make the most of their participation on the team.

When they enter the game, they know that they have the chance to be difference-makers, but at the same time, they are willing to give others around them the opportunity shine. You can see this when these stars pass the ball to the other players as opposed to expecting others to pass to them first.

This attitude is what can certainly make, or break, the overall performance of your team. So, please be aware that your choice of Scrum Master is just as important as any other team member you need to choose. Your choice for Scrum Master needs to be as committed, or even more so, than the rest of the members of the project team.

At the end of the day, everyone is on the same boat. No more, no less. So, it's worth making the most of their time on the boat.

Chapter 6: Running a sprint

At this point, you should have all of your project planning done and your Scrum team all set and ready to go. So, the biggest issue now becomes getting your project off the ground.

Scrum, as compared to other project management methodologies, breaks a project's development into sections called "sprints." For experienced Scrum practitioners, sprints represent intermediate steps that build on each other. Consequently, the process by which the project team is able to build the final outcome allows for a gradual and incremental approach in building the project.

This is an important aspect to take into account since building the project progressively allows the project team to consider which aspects are susceptible to improvement as each sprint wears on.

In that sense, each one of the sprints produces an outcome which then serves as the basis for the next sprint. However, each sprint also allows the Scrum team to consider the mistakes and problems encountered as a part of the previous sprint.

This is one of the key differences in Scrum as opposed other non-agile project management methodologies. When you run a project through a series of successive sprints, you are able to correct the mistakes, bugs and any other issues before the final testing of the product.

This is a direct byproduct of the Agile manifesto.

In the Agile manifesto, working software and value to the customer are an essential part of the process throughout the entire lifecycle of the project.

So, that implies that the project team must be able to deliver value to the customer at the end of each sprint. While "working software" refers specifically to an IT or software-related project, the concept of delivering value at the end of each sprint represents a cross-cutting approach which can be applied to any project.

Consider this example:

A construction company is building a road. For the sake of simplicity, the company has broken down a 10-mile road into 10, one-mile sprints. As such, the outcome of each sprint is intended to deliver a one-mile stretch of road which is perfectly usable at the end of the sprint.

So, this implies that at the end of all 10 sprints, the entire road will be completed.

Thus, the end of each, individual sprint delivers "working software," in this case, a road.

Under traditional project management methodologies, the value to the customer would not be delivered until the end of the project, that is, at the end of all 10 miles. While this is a traditional approach utilized with projects such as road construction, the fact of the matter is that is there was a design flaw, or some other type of mistake during the construction process, it wouldn't be addressed until the end of the project. This is why it is so common to have construction projects delivered only to find flaws and design issues.

Once the project is completed, correcting issues may be virtually impossible. As such, construction projects may end becoming useless since it is too late to address any potential issues. This is why it is common to find that public works end up becoming costly mistakes.

So, when it comes time to getting your project off the ground, it certainly pays to take the time to really plan out the activities which will be conducted in each sprint and how this can be utilized to get deliver value to the customer as early as possible in the project's lifecycle. While this means that you may not be able to deliver working software at the end of the very first sprint, you might be able to deliver value very early on as opposed to waiting all the way to the end of the project to do so.

Envisioning

In this first step of the planning process, the project's vision may be created. This is where the Product Owner sits down and puts the project's vision together. So, this may imply that you, as a Product Owner, or as a project sponsor, will think about where the project should be headed.

At this point, the Product Canvas really becomes a useful tool.

In an earlier chapter, we described how the Product Canvas can be utilized to develop a vision which can be "sold" to potential team members. This project vision is vital in getting the people on board for the project. If you are not able to articulate your vision in a tangible and visual manner, your project may well be doomed from the start.

When you are developing your vision, the Product Canvas becomes the springboard for the final product's development. The Product Canvas will be able to help you determine what needs to be done, when it needs to be done and for whom it needs to be done. So, let's drill down on some of the finer points of the Product Canvas which were not discussed in the previous chapter.

Product Name

The final output of your product needs to have a name. Whatever it is, it will most likely be called something. So, determining that name early one is useful, but not an absolute necessity.

Think of films and books.

Often, films and books have a working title. This is the title by which writers have produced the original draft or script by which the film is shot, or the book is edited.

Somewhere along the way, a director or studio executive may choose to change the title. Perhaps there's a line or scene in the movie which provides the inspiration for the final name of the film. Perhaps there is an event in the movie's production that forces the name change. Perhaps it boils down to marketing and how marketing the movie is much easier under a different title. Whatever the case, the working title may end up being dropped in favor for a different title.

The same thing happens with book publishers. Often, publishers may not be enamored with the title of a book and choose to change it during the editing process. While writers may not agree with the title, it is the ultimate decision on the part of the publisher since they are the ones who will be printing the book.

In that regard, your product's name may be changed as a result of the development process. Perhaps your Development Team may come up with a better, cleverer name for the product. It might end up being better than you could have imagined. Or, it could be that you just couldn't think of a name, and as a result of the development process, your team has come up with a good one.

In the end, whatever you choose to call the work in progress should give your team a clear idea of what they are working on. Something vague such as "Project X" won't cut it. Unless you are working on a top-secret military project, your best bet is to find a working title that makes sense to your team. So, if you are developing a fitness app, a good working title might be, "Fit 2 go." If that sounds corny, your team can always come up with something different.

The project vision

So, the use of the Product Canvas is all about generating the vision for the project. However, it is often useful, and necessary, to articulate your product's vision into one statement which encompasses the entire value being developed throughout the project lifecycle.

Consequently, you may have a project statement such as, "bridging two communities." This statement would apply to actually building a physical bridge between two communities, or perhaps bridging communication between two communities. In either case, you are making an emphasis on the fact that you are bridging communication. No more, no less.

The canvas itself allows all stakeholders to have a clear idea of where the project is going at all times.

How the canvas is actually presented depends on the nature of the product and of the stakeholder. Personally, I like to have two versions. One, a digital version which can be shared through Google Docs or some other type of file sharing format. The other could be a print version which can be displayed on a board or pinned up on a wall.

In either case, the canvas should be visible to everyone so that they are able to have a constant reminder of where they are going and what the end result of the project is going to be. Also, having the canvas up on display will allow everyone to be constantly reminded of what they are working toward. It is incredible how having a constant reminder of what you should be doing and why you are doing it allows you to keep your focus while reducing the likelihood of distraction. It also helps the project team to cut out any tasks that are not related to the individual sprint or the project itself.

Product Backlog and sprint backlog

Once the project vision has been developed and properly shared, it is time to develop the Product Backlog.

The Product Backlog is essentially a collection of all of the tasks which will be completed throughout the lifecycle of the project leading up to the ultimate completion of the final product. The Product Backlog depends on the number of sprints that will be run and the amount of time each sprint will last.

These parameters are not standard and really depend on the aspects of each project. For instance, you might have four weeks to complete a project. And, given the scope of the project, you might feel that one, four-week sprint would be enough to get the job done.

In other cases, the customer may leave it up to you decide how long the project will take. So, you could approach it in one of two ways.

Firstly, you base your decision on your experience. You have done similar projects in the past. So, you are aware of how long it will take to get the job done given a certain set of conditions. This might be your most accurate way of measuring how long the final product will take especially if you don't have specific time constraints.

The second approach could be to have your project team assembled and make the decision based on a realistic assessment of all of the project members. In this case, you would take everyone's opinions into account in order to determine what needs to be done and when it should be done.

Under this approach, you would determine the number of sprints, the length of each sprint and then proceed to create the Product Backlog based on the feedback given by your team. Ultimately, you would be able to determine the tempo at which the project would be run and what kind of pace your team would need in order to get the job done within the time frame they have decided.

So, if you have a team that works faster as compared to other comparable teams, you may be confident in reducing the time needed in order to get the project done. In other cases, you might have a more inexperienced group which would motivate you to take on more time to complete the final outcome.

A good rule of thumb is that sprints generally last from two to four weeks. Given that all projects are different, the project team would have to figure out what the best length for a sprint would be. As such, a two-week sprint might work best, or perhaps a six-week sprint. It all depends on what the actual project is about. But on the whole, a good rule of thumb seems to be four weeks.

My advice would be to consult sprint lengths with your team whenever possible. Unless you have time and / or budgetary constraints that limit the amount of time you have to complete a project, the best way to go about it would be to ask your team how fast they could get the job done and base your timing decisions on that.

Learn fast and pivot

Often, there will be mistakes made in the early stages of a project. This is especially true when you are not familiar with a particular type of project. So, it is always a good idea to fail early and get those mistakes out of the way. In doing so, you will be able to find your bearing early on. The worst thing that can happen is not addressing issues early on only to have them grow into something much larger in the latter stages of the project. So, it is always best to be willing to fail early on and learn the lessons which will allow your team to get the most out of their experience.

One very important point is that tolerance to failure should be seen as the result of a learning experience. This tolerance is based on the normal course of business in a project. However, truly, large-scale mistakes should be avoided at all costs.

Consider this situation:

Your team is designing a new car. The requests from the customer call for a lighter vehicle which you have a smaller engine and thereby improving fuel economy. So, your design team comes up with a lighter frame which enables it to put in a smaller engine. However, initial estimates were off, and the car actually weighs more than intended. And since you chose a smaller engine, it now turns out that the car doesn't have the same power and acceleration as originally intended. But since this project was conducted under a traditional project management methodology, the team didn't realize this mistake until the first prototypes were built.

When the results of the initial testing were brought forth to the company executives, they were given two choices. One, go back to the drawing board and alter the frame, or put in a bigger engine. The company executives decided to axe the project as they felt safety features would be compromised by a lighter frame and putting a bigger engine in would not meet the fuel economy standards that the company wants to offer its customers. So, by axing the project, the work done by this team goes up in smoke.

In this example, the team made a catastrophic mistake which led to the demise of the project at the testing phase. Had someone caught on to that mistake early on, then the project might well have been saved. But since they didn't, the project was a complete failure.

With this example, the intent is to provide a greater understanding of how a project should be managed given the circumstances which it might be under. As such, failure, so long as it does not jeopardize the project itself, should be taken in stride.

Great sprint planning

Now that you have the overall scheme of where your project is headed, it's time to plan your first sprint. In order to plan a sprint, the Scrum team takes part in what is known as the Sprint Planning Meeting.

During this meeting, the Scrum team creates the Sprint Backlog. The Sprint Backlog feed off the original Product Backlog, that is, it chooses which tasks from the overall Product Backlog will be completed in that sprint.

Naturally, the first sprint would have all tasks available to it. This would mean that the Scrum team needs to be very careful in deciding which tasks will get done first. If you are planning subsequent sprints, then you would have a reduced number of tasks available given that some might have already been completed.

With that in mind, the Sprint Planning Meeting provides the team with the tasks that will go into the work breakdown structure that actually tells individual team members what they will do in each sprint.

The Scrum Master can then track progress on the Scrum board and the Scrum Burndown Chart. The Burndown Chart is simply a visual tool which tells the team how much time there is left before the sprint is completed. This allows the Scrum team to focus and not waste any time.

As such, the Sprint Backlog provides the team with the objectives it needs to complete at the end of the sprint. It is simply up to the Scrum Master to make sure that progress stays on track throughout the duration of the sprint.

Release planning

Since the aim of each sprint is to produce working software, there needs to be a set of criteria which would determine what needs to be done in order to achieve a product release. This could be a set of criteria which determine the functionality of the product.

Consider this example.

The team is developing a new medication. At the end of a sprint, the new medication will be ready for animal testing. However, it needs to meet the technical criteria determined to be needed in order to have it approved by the official government regulatory agency for animal testing. If these criteria are not met, then the drug will not be approved for animal testing and the deadline will not be met. On the other hand, if the deadline is met, then the drug will proceed on to the next stage and everyone comes up a winner.

This end result can only be achieved by careful track of the project's progress and grooming of the backlog. This implies that the backlog will reflect what has already been done and what needs to be completed. At the end of the day, the remaining tasks will reflect the need of the project based on the overall conditions the project is under.

The example of a new medication underscores one very important aspect: certain projects will have to meet with requirements that go beyond any requirements the customer can make. Rather, those requirements may come from government agencies or regulatory bodies. In which case, the project team needs to have that in mind in order to determine the project's overall success rate.

Furthermore, each sprint should get closer and closer to the ultimate release of the final, finished version of the product. Thus, when the final product is eventually released, it will be fully compliant with all requirements thereby greatly reducing the chance that the project will not pass the standards it will be held up against.

Optimizing a sprint

As with anything in Scrum, it is subject to optimization. That means that there is always room for continuous improvement. Even if you think that something cannot be improved, there is always some room from improved functionality.

As such, running a sprint is no different.

First off, the Daily Standup Meeting provides an opportunity for feedback on a daily basis. This implies that the Scrum team would have a chance to go over their daily work and see where things may be improved, or perhaps cut out, based on the fact that there are mistakes or negative conditions to be rectified.

The Daily Standup Meeting also allows for team members to voice any concerns about the direction the project is headed and what can be done to deal with such situations. Perhaps there is a team member that is not pulling their weight. Or, one piece of vital equipment is not working properly. Perhaps there are unforeseen circumstances which are holding the team back. Whatever the case, this meeting allows for feedback on a daily basis.

So, it's important for the team to create a feedback loop. The Scrum Master may provide feedback on the way they see how things are going while the team can provide feedback based on their perception of the way things are going. The main thing to keep in mind is that there is no need to be afraid of feedback, rather, it is certainly worthwhile to be honest and forthcoming about the way things are going. At the end of the day, feedback allows for assessment and greater understanding of how the overall process is going.

The Sprint Review Meeting

Once the end of a sprint has been reached, the team will hold what is known as the Sprint Review Meeting. In this meeting, the team will present their latest advancements to the customer. The customer will then be able to see the product's functionality at that stage of the project.

For example, the project is at a point where the project is ready to be tested, but it does not have the full set of features that the final version of the product will have.

Consider the example of a car.

The car has been fully built and can be road tested. The car is fully functional in the sense that it has a frame, powertrain and certain safety features, but does not include the full set of features such as the final paint job, accessories and other electronics. The reason for conducting a road test at the end of the sprint is to show the customer what the vehicle can do in terms of its performance. In later sprints, the full range of features will be added so that the customer can see what the finished product will look like.

At this point, the customer can give their blessing so the team can move on to the next stage, or perhaps critique the release of the product so that the team can go back and make changes as per the customer's request.

The main purpose of this meeting is to get feedback. Of course, if everything is perfect, then there would be no need to worry about changes to the product. But if feedback suggests there should be changes made, then the team still have time to right the ship before the final release of the product.

The Sprint Retrospect Meeting

During the Sprint Retrospect Meeting, the Scrum team has the chance to sit down and go over what was done, and what wasn't, during the previous sprint. This is a space for open and honest commentary so that each member is aware of what they are doing, and how they could improve upon their work.

In addition, it also allows for the customer's feedback during the Sprint Review Meeting to be incorporated in the upcoming Sprint Planning Meeting. While there may be a number of issues to discuss, the Sprint Retrospect Meeting, as all meetings in Scrum, should be short and to the point. Once the main issues have been cleared up, then the Sprint Planning Meeting should incorporate the reflections and feedback from the previous sprint.

Personally, I like to have the Sprint Retrospect Meeting segue into the Sprint Planning Meeting as all of the items discussed are fresh and at the forefront of everyone's minds. If you choose to let some time in between both meetings, you might end up missing the point of the feedback your received. Thus, it is always a good idea to address issues while they are fresh in everyone's minds.

Once you have gone through feedback and any issues Scrum team members encountered in previous sprints, you would then be ready to kick off your next sprint. And then, the entire process repeats itself. This is why Scrum is considered to be iterative as the same process repeats itself over several times throughout the course of the project's lifecycle.

Ultimately, your efforts to foster continuous improvement stem from your ability to take the feedback which has been provided to you by your customer and team and incorporate it to your planning down the road. In doing this, you are ensuring that your team feels that their voices are being heard while you can rest assured that you are trying to your best to address any and all potential issues before they become a potential problem.

Chapter 7: Scaling up Scrum

One of the biggest criticisms is that Scrum is not scalable. That means, that it is not suited for large projects. However, that criticism is unfounded, and it is rooted in a lack of knowledge and understanding on how Agile works.

Agile essentially works like any other project management methodology. If there is a large-scale project which needs to be completed, it can be blown up to meet such proportions. If the project is small and does not require a vast amount of resources, then Agile and Scrum can suit those small projects, too.

The reason for this belief is that Agile was born out of the software industry. So, many non-Scrum practitioners believe that Scrum cannot be scaled and thereby lacks the necessary elements of truly large projects.

Well, what would count as a large project?

How about constructing a building?

A building, as a structure, has several elements and components. For example, digging up the land, laying the foundation, building the structure, doing the interior, electrical, plumbing and roofing, and any other specific components such as elevators or escalators.

Every one of the components previously mentioned could well be run by an individual Scrum team. For instance, the foundation requires a considerable amount of manpower and resources to complete. So, your construction site supervisor can work as a Scrum Master. The supervisor would be to use each of their individual construction workers as members of the Development Team. Each member has their own role to play and will provide their own contributions to the project.

Now, the Scrum Master, or supervisor, reports to the project engineer (the Product Owner) who is in constant touch with the customer and project sponsors. This communication allows all of the stakeholders in the process to know if the project is on track or falling behind.

Once the foundation has been laid down, the same group of workers could transition into the structure team. Perhaps these workers are specialists in laying down foundations and would not be a part of the structure team. In which case, the structure team would be a separate Scrum team. In any event, there is a supervisor acting as a Scrum Master with the project engineer acting as the Product Owner.

Also, it could be that each sprint corresponds to one floor being built. So, the project team estimates that it can finish a floor in a week. So, if the building has 15 floors, then the structure itself would take 15 weeks.

Then, another Scrum team, the electrical and plumbing would come in and set everything up. They also estimate that they would be done with one floor per week. However, the are not going to wait until the structure team is done. They will get started once the first floor is done. That way, the interior team will be one week behind the structure team.

Now, the customer can be called in at the end of each sprint, that is, once the foundation has been laid. And then, after the structure on the first floor is done and then after the interior has been done and so on. In reality, the customer only needs to see one floor once as the remaining floors would all be the same.

This example clearly underscores how Scrum is not only adaptable to any industry, but it can be scaled as needed.

In fact, when the construction project reaches a point where multiple Scrum teams are working at once, the project engineer will have multiple supervisors working at the same time. This makes the project engineer the Project Product Owner. The Project Product Owner may choose to name a Project Scrum Master, which would be one Scrum Master coordinating the work of the individual Scrum Masters.

And just like any other Scrum project, there are Sprint Review Meetings and Sprint Retrospect Meetings. In this example, the supervisor can call his workers in for a short meeting and just go over any issues they may be having. For instance, the weather isn't cooperating, and workers are being negatively affected by it.

Such simple aspects can go a long way toward providing useful feedback thus ensuring the overall quality of the project.

Scrum of Scrums

When dealing with larger Scrum teams, a technique called a "Scrum of Scrums" can be used in order to manage the daily tasks of such a large group. Unlike the previous example, a Scrum of Scrums does not have multiple teams with multiple Scrum Masters. This concept considers having one large team which is divided into subgroups. This plays off the initial consideration we had about maintaining ever-numbered groups.

Let's consider the following case.

A Scrum team consists of 16 members given the size and the scope of the project to be completed. The budgetary restrictions do not allow for individual Scrum teams, say, two teams of eight, or even three teams of six. So, there is one Scrum Master and one Product Owner looking after all 16 members.

In order to make the division of labor much easier, the Scrum Master has divided the 16 members into four subgroups of four. Each subgroup is intended to cover a specific amount of work during each sprint.

Since the Scrum team has a Daily Standup Meeting, the Scrum Master has to make a choice: does the Daily Standup Meeting include all 16 members of the team or could the meeting include less members?

There is one problem with each approach.

In this first approach, having all 16 members may drag out the meeting far longer than necessary. Each member may have something to say and that, in itself, may lead to some disorganization in the meeting. So, the meeting could ultimately become counterproductive.

The second approach, working with less individuals poses a problem since it would be difficult to choose who is in the meeting and who isn't. One workaround could be to designate a "group lead" and have this person attend the daily meetings. That would reduce the amount of participants from 16 to 4. But that poses another issue: Scrum does not advocate "leaders" or folks "in charge" within each group. Bear in mind that Scrum has a flat structure meaning that everyone has equal participation.

So, what's the solution?

A Scrum of Scrums.

JEFF COHN

In a Scrum of Scrums, each of the members of the subgroup gets a chance to represent the team at the daily meeting. Since everyone is equally involved in the process, everyone would be equally qualified to represent the group at the meeting. A good rule of thumb is to rotate reps every day. Unless sprints were unusually long, rotating reps every day makes the most sense.

Now, it could be that a sprint would take 8 weeks. In such a case, the team might decide to rotate reps on a weekly basis. That might work insofar as giving each member the opportunity to handle the responsibility of attending the meeting on a more permanent basis.

Now, the one consideration under this approach is to avoid having one "permanent" rep. The whole point of avoiding a permanent person representing the group boils down to avoiding having any semblance of hierarchy within the Scrum team. As such, having a rotating representation is the best way to go.

Ultimately, the point of having such a set up is to reduce the likelihood of one team member taking over the rest of the group. While there are folks who are more naturally inclined to a leadership role, the fact of the matter is that

146

by having rotating roles, you are able to make sure that everyone gets equal participation thereby fostering a collaborative approach within the team.

Scaled Agile framework

So, when Agile is scaled up to a larger framework, keeping track of the workflow and making sure that the collaborative nature sticks gets harder and harder. So, it then becomes a challenge for Scrum practitioners to enforce a discipline whereby team members have equal participation, work is conducted in as per the user stories outlined at the beginning of the sprint, and the overall nature of the project is completed within the aspects pertaining to the Agile mindset.

As such, large projects can be perfectly accommodated within an Agile framework with the basic difference that the ultimate work breakdown structure as seen in the Product Backlog and the individual Sprint Backlogs may be divided among individual teams rather than one collective work divided among individual team members.

In order to make this concept resonate on a deeper level, consider the following situation:

A food manufacturer wants to produce a new low-calorie drink. Since the market is demanding low-calorie drink options, the management team at this corporation is looking to produce a low-calorie drink which can compete with other brands in similar categories.

Consequently, a team has been assembled in order to determine the right formula for this new drink. The company has decided to invest in research and development into producing a new drink rather than just rebadging an existing one.

So, the CEO of the company has called in one of the company's production engineers and named them "project engineer." This engineer is aware of the value in the adoption of a Scrum approach to this project. As such, the project engineer has assumed the role of Scrum Master. The client is the CEO who has been designated by the company's board as the person in charge of making sure the project comes to fruition.

Thus, the project engineer comes in a decides to build multiple Scrum teams that can work at once especially since the company has determined that a proposal for a new drink needs to be ready before the holiday season. In this case, the project would have about three months to be completed. This means that there is no time to be wasted.

The Scrum Master, or project engineer, decides that the best course of action is to assemble a research team which can look into the actual production of the drink, a production team which can look into the logistics of bottling and distribution and a marketing team which can come up with a brand name, graphics and art for the sole purpose of producing the new drink.

All three teams will work in tandem in such a way that they are all in a concerted effort toward producing a new, low-calorie drink.

The Scrum Master has decided to coordinate each team through a Scrum of Scrums approach. Under this approach, the main idea is to ensure that the all of the teams are working in tandem thus moving the project along with multiple groups working in sync.

In every sprint, each of the groups works on the same user story, except from their own angle. So, the user story is based on a consumer who is young and is looking for a low-calorie option which can help them cut down on their sugar consumption while maintaining the flavor of other drinks on the market.

At the end of each sprint, all three teams present their advances. The research team presents their results in the development of the drink, the production team indicates how they will approach the product while the marketing team unveils their plans for the drink.

Ultimately, the entire team arrives at the same destination with a finished drink, distribution and production considerations in check, and a solid marketing campaign in place. The final presentation of the product is presented to the company's board. The project is approved by the board and is ready for an official product release, that is, a formal launch into the marketplace.

This example underscores the fact that in order to tackle a rather large project, the project engineer, or Scrum Master, decided to find the best way to come up with a new drink and set it up in the market. Whether or not the product is a success once in the market remains to be seen. The most important thing to keep in mind is the need for the project team to find the best way to work on the project in a collaborative manner which underscores the needs and requests of the customer thus delivering value at all times.

Coordinating multiple Scrum teams

In the previous example, we were able to see how multiple Scrum teams can be coordinated through the use of a Scrum of Scrums. While using multiple Scrum Masters might be a good solution, it might not be the most practical when taking budgetary restrictions. The previous example highlighted how the company wanted a new low-calorie drink and just tapped one of their best engineers to take on the project.

While the project engineer could have found a traditional approach and used a regular methodology to exert influence, the fact is that the new drink might not have been ready in time for the launch. The reason for this is the interdependency among tasks. Under a traditional approach, the project team would have to wait for one team to be done before the next team could begin.

Sure, this approach would provide a more "predictable" outcome, the fact of the matter is that traditional project management methodologies are used to produce predictable results. When something such as the creation of a new product requires the intervention of a project team, then there is a clear need for the each of the members to find the best way to make their work count. That is why Scrum can be used across a number of different industries and fields.

The fact that Scrum has a cross-cutting appeal, it allows project managers to find an effective way of running a number of teams simultaneously. This implies that the project team is able to make sense of the various tasks that need to be done in such a way that the project team is able to get a firm grasp on the various objectives that need to be completed throughout the lifecycle of the project.

Moreover, being able to use Scrum in a scalable fashion allows for greater flexibility as opposed to a rigid, traditional project management approach that forces project managers to delay certain portions of a project until one portion is complete.

For instance, a traditional project management methodology would not allow all three teams to run simultaneously. The project team would have to wait until there was a successful formula developed for the drink while the remaining teams might be able to come up with ideas but wouldn't be able to work until the previous step had been developed.

Distributed Scrum teams

One of the most important factors in a Scrum project is finding the right way to manage multiple teams working at the same time. Ideally, these teams would be distributed evenly at the same physical location. This is the concept of co-location, and according to Scrum doctrine, it is the best way in order to ensure that teams are working collaboratively.

But what happens if there are teams distributed in different geographical locations?

Is it possible to run a sprint when team members are not physically located in the same place?

The answer is yes.

Modern technology has facilitated communication in such a way that teams can work in different geographical locations and still achieve positive results. The fact that Scrum teams can communicate via the internet allows for teams to work remotely without having to bridge the distance by moving and thereby increasing the cost of the project.

However, such an approach is not for everyone.

JEFF COHN

Some folks can work perfectly fine on their own. They are capable of producing results without having someone looking over their shoulder to see what they are doing. Then, there are others who are not so adept at working on their own. They may find themselves in a situation in which they need to have someone telling them what to do in order to get things done.

While Scrum does not advocate telling people what to do, the psychological pressure of having a team working around them helps them to focus on getting work done. Nevertheless, using Scrum to work with teams located in different geographical locations is possible.

Yet, there is one limitation. Such projects need to be those which can be assembled over the internet, or which do not require the production of a physical good. In such cases, there would be a point where team members would have to come together to produce the actual, physical good.

Consequently, part of the project could be done remotely, and part of the project would have to be done in person. Under these circumstances, project teams would be able to make sense of their tasks without necessarily having to be together at all times.

How and when this approach is used depends largely on the nature of the project. So, it's up to the project manager to find the right way to make sure that the project team can work despite distance and other considerations that may negatively affect the team's overall performance.

The use of Scrum in maintenance projects

At this point of the book, we have discussed how Scrum is used to create value especially when there are new products being produced. Yet, we have not discussed what happens in the case of such projects where there is nothing new being created, but maintenance is the primary focus.

One such example could be an update to an existing product. This update could be commissioned by the customer or stakeholder in order to fix bugs found in a project.

Consider this situation:

An automobile manufacturer has realized that one of their recent models has been shown to have transmission problems. So, the automobile manufacturer has decided to commission a Scrum team to find a good solution to the transmission issues for this vehicle.

In this example, the project team is not actually developing anything new. They are just finding corrective measures to a problem which has been identified after the release of the final product. Now, you might think, "why wasn't the problem detected?"

The reason for something such as this could be due to the fact that testing did not reflect the true conditions under which the final product was going to be used. So, even though the initial project team tested the new car's transmission, they were unable to determine how well it would hold up under normal circumstances.

The end result was the need to fix the transmission for upcoming models to be released.

The Scrum team has come together, run several sprints, detected the problem and proposed a corrective solution. The latter sprints were intended to provide more thorough testing to the new transmission so as to avoid the same problems the previous transmission had. In the end, the results were positive, and the new transmission has been cleared for new models.

This example underscores how it is possible to use Scrum even when you are not exactly producing anything new. It could be that fixing a faulty transmission required a minor tweak in the overall design of the device. Nevertheless, a Scrum team was able to find it and make sense of how it can be improved.

Bear in mind that Scrum is all about continuous improvement. So, these types of projects are specifically aimed at producing such continuous development, not just in the production of new projects, but in improving upon existing ones.

Conclusion

So, we have arrived at the end of this journey through the world of Scrum and Agile. I hope that you have found this book to be useful and informative.

If you have made it this far it is because you are truly interested in making the most of your experience as a Scrum practitioner. If you are new to the Agile world, then I am sure you have walked away with a greater and deeper understanding of how Agile can become a feasible way in which you can produce high-impact projects in a logical and congruent manner.

As such, I would encourage you to get your feet wet in the world of Agile. I assure you that once you see how effective Agile can be, you will not go back. Scrum is the most powerful Agile methodology you can find today. It is not only the ultimate concentration of viable projects, but also the best way in which you can find the means to produce results that will make your projects successful every time you take the field.

As always, please don't forget to comment on this book. There are other interested folks who are looking to learn more about Agile and Scrum, and how these methodologies can help them improve their own knowledge and acumen in the project management world.

Also, please share this information with your colleagues and business associates, or anyone who would be interested in the world of Agile. I am sure that they will find this book to be useful in helping them build their own understanding of the Agile world and how they can improve their own projects. I am sure that they will appreciate learning from you as well.

See you next time.

Made in the USA
Monee, IL
14 November 2019